Praise for END MEDICAL DEBT

End Medical Debt confronts an important, sad truth: No one asks to be sick. It's hard enough being poor; it's hard enough being sick. But being poor and sick becomes a death sentence for some, a life sentence of indentured servitude for others. The bills are almost beyond belief. I went into the hospital overnight with chest pains, and the hospital bill was $25,000. It's time to lift this yoke off the necks of some of the most vulnerable and defenseless members of society — and that is precisely what *End Medical Debt* does.

    Alan Grayson
    Former U.S. Congressman (D-FL)

End Medical Debt does more than describe the unsustainable structure of our current health care system. The book demonstrates what was always the solution: People helping people, voluntarily and without coercion. The current healthcare system has created a debt-enslaved class with few options. Necessity will produce many solutions, but in the meantime, *End Medical Debt* is offering hope from those willing and able to pay forward their success. Humanity at its best.

    Ernest Hancock
    Publisher, FreedomsPhoenix
    Talk Show Host, "Declare Your Independence"

End Medical Debt explains that among all the developed countries, only Americans risk the probability that medical treatment will be financially inaccessible or that a family will be made destitute from a serious injury or disease. The sacrifices families make for medical care of loved ones is heartbreaking. The experience and wisdom of authors Jerry Ashton, Robert Goff and Craig Antico have resulted in the system presented in their exciting new book. Their charity, RIP Medical Debt, may well help us to turn the corner on this major problem facing quality medical care in America.

    Nancy A. Niparko, M.D
    Diplomate, American Board of Psychiatry & Neurology
    Attending Neurologist, Children's Hospital Los Angeles

While care providers fight to make ends meet and corporate interests seek out profit margins everywhere, politicians struggle to strike a balance as more and more Americans are compounding their serious health issues with unprecedented and unmanageable medical debt. Meanwhile, a small self-appointed group of experts from the world of health care finance are seeking solutions for consumers, providers and a broken system. Where there are no acceptable answers yet, people are creating them. Jerry Ashton, Robert Goff and Craig Antico are putting lifetimes of experience to work in *End Medical Debt* to spread the word that medical debt is a personal and national crisis. More so, they are offering answers that are gaining national attention.

    Kevin A. Cahill
    New York State Assemblyman (District 103)
    Chair, Assembly Committee on Insurance
    Member, Assembly Committee on Health

End Medical Debt is exactly what is needed to jumpstart the much-needed national discussion about our current dysfunctional for-profit health care system, and what to do about it, so patients like me don't have to experience the financial and personal hardships caused by medical debt. We are a forgotten, disposable, invisible universe of people. There are millions of us. This book explains with passion and honesty the nightmare of medical debt.

    Joel R. Segal
    Former senior legislative assistant, U.S. Congress, 2000-2019,
    Co-author, HR 676: "Expanded and Improved Medicare For All"

END MEDICAL DEBT

Of all the forms of inequality, injustice in health is the most shocking and inhumane.

— Martin Luther King, Jr.

END MEDICAL DEBT

Curing America's $1 Trillion Unpayable Healthcare Debt

Jerry Ashton
Robert Goff
Craig Antico
Founders of RIP Medical Debt

Edited by Judah Freed

Kauai, Hawaii USA

END MEDICAL DEBT

Publisher Website: HokuHouse.com
RIP Website: RIPmedicaldebt.org

Editor, Cover & Book Designer: Judah Freed

Published by Hoku House, Kauai, Hawaii
Printed in the United States of America.
eBook in mobi and epub formats.

    Cloth Hardcover: ISBN-13: 978-0-9892241-0-9
    Trade Softcover: ISBN-13: 978-0-9892241-2-3
    eBook: ISBN-13: 978-0-9892241-1-6

Please contact the publisher at HokuHouse.com for special orders.

© Copyright 2018 by Jerry Ashton, Robert Goff and Craig Antico. All rights reserved.

No portion of this book may be reproduced or transmitted by any means, electronic or mechanical — including photocopying, faxing, recording, or by any information storage and retrieval system, e.g., Internet website or academic eReserves — without explicit permission from the publisher. Reviewers may quote passages under Fair Use.

The opinions expressed by each individual author are not necessarily those of the other authors, RIP Medical Debt and its supporters, or the publisher.

This book contains information intended to help readers become better informed consumers of health care and citizens active in public discourse. The book is not intended as a substitute for the advice of a licensed physician or certified financial counselor. The reader is advised to consult with a trusted professional for all matters relating to personal health and finances.

First edition published on December 7, 2018.

Library of Congress Control Number: (Pending)
Cataloging-in-Publication Data:

Ashton, Jerry, 1937 —
Goff, Robert, 1952 —
Antico, Craig, 1961 —
    END MEDICAL DEBT
    Curing America's $1 Trillion Unpayable Healthcare Debt

195 pages with 11 Chapters.

    1. Contemporary Affairs. 2. Personal Finance.
    3. Politics/Government. 4. Health 5. Economics.

Dedication

For all who struggle with medical debt
and for all who care to abolish it.

An institution or reform movement that is not selfish, must originate in the recognition of some evil that is adding to the sum of human suffering, or diminishing the sum of happiness.

— Clara Barton

END MEDICAL DEBT

Table of Contents

Acknowledgements	ix
Preface: **A Meeting of Minds** *Judah Freed*	xi
1. **Seeing Through the Tears** *Jerry Ashton*	3
2. **Medical Debt Is the Enemy of Everyone** *Robert Goff*	15
3. **Debt Mountains Cause Healthcare Deserts** *Craig Antico*	37
4. **The John Oliver Effect** *Jerry Ashton*	49
5. **Debt Is in the Details** *Craig Antico*	67
6. **Margin over Mission: Head vs Heart** *Robert Goff*	79
7. **Fanciful Healthcare Financing** *Robert Goff*	97

8.	**No Thank You for Your Service** *Jerry Ashton*	119
9.	**Health Is a Goal, Not an Industry** *Robert Goff*	131
10.	**Personal and General Medical Debt Solutions** *Craig Antico*	145
11.	**National Healthcare: To Be or Not To Be?** *Jerry Ashton*	163

About the Authors	179
About RIP Medical Debt	181

Acknowledgements

The three authors of *End Medical Debt* each have great people to thank for helping them to create this book.

Jerry Ashton: My fullest expression of gratitude goes to my co-authors and the publisher, without whose efforts this book and the success of RIP Medical Debt would not have happened. First in line after them is my wife, Kate Coburn, and my wonderful daughters, Andrea and Alexandra, for their unfailing support. They have been my anchor in every storm. The magnetic center of influence in my personal and professional growth has been Occupy Wall Street and my experience with its famous "Rolling Jubilee" experiment in debt forgiveness, which inspired our charity. Occupy was the petri dish in which many ideas and solutions could develop and mature, RIP being one of them. Here's to all you Occupiers, past and present, who caused me to be aware and then motivated me to put that awareness into responsible action. *End Medical Debt* is dedicated to your continuing and important influence in America

Robert Goff: My contributions to the book would not be possible without my immersion for over 45 years in the American healthcare system. Nearly 20 years with the University Physicians Network gave me insights to practitioners of the art and science of medical practice with care and compassion. Such leaders as doctors Stuart Garay, Sol Zimmerman and Paula Marchetta are examples. I'm grateful for a decade of collaboration with Edward Ullman to create and operate one of New York's earliest HMOs, trying to offer both quality and affordability in health care coverage. The variety of roles during my career contributed different perspectives. My wife Jinny and my son Blake's experience as healthcare consumers have kept me grounded in the actual patient experience within the disjointed healthcare non-system. I also want to acknowledge my co-authors, Jerry Ashton and Craig Antico, for their energy and creativity in forming RIP Medical Debt, whose mission this book seeks to support.

Craig Antico: I wish to thank: Jerry Ashton, progressive activist and gadfly (my balance) turned partner, friend and wise mentor; you haven't changed; but, thanks to you, I have. Jessica, spouse of great sacrifice, giver, cheerleader, loyal best friend, an intelligent, caring, conservative influence. My uniquely caring sons Erik, Clark, Alex, Connor, and Chad. My optimistic and well-read father, Al. Mother Barbara never gave up on me! Andy Goldstone, using TransUnion data for good through RIP. Albert Handy, an unselfish supporter, idea creator, inspiring me to build the most compassionate, life-changing, unbiased, impactful donor-led charity platform for good ever funded, designed and implemented. Fergus Cloughley and Paul Wallis: true partners and friends, inventors of data flow science. Dan Love, pastor, nurturing my faith in God, compassion for community. Robert Goff, storyteller and teacher. Matt Maloney. Bill York, visionary, networking communities for wellness. Judah Freed, our sagacious editor. Researchers Francis Wong, Ray Kluender, Wes Yin, and Neale Mahoney for rigorous, evidence-based insight.

Judah Freed: I thank my wife Melissa Mojo, all three authors, the RIP team, ProofreadingQueen, IBPA, and publicist ally Ilene Proctor.

We all thank *you* for actually reading acknowledgments!

PREFACE

A Meeting of Minds

Judah Freed, Editor

Have you ever heard the one about the progressive, the moderate and the conservative who walked into a charity? They forgive medical debt, and they wrote this book on how the U.S. healthcare system has created *$1 trillion* in unpayable medical debt. They agree on the economic causes. They disagree on the solutions. Well, all the solutions save a simple act of charity: Abolish uncollectible medical debt by buying it and forgiving it!

All three authors of *End Medical Debt* are medical debt industry insiders. Together they began RIP Medical Debt, a tax-exempt charity that locates, buys and forgives unpayable medical bills.

They see debt forgiveness as necessary but not sufficient, our best interim solution until we can agree on a better financial structure for the U.S. healthcare system. This book is a step in that direction.

End Medical Debt presents a clear "big picture" of medical debt with pragmatic insights on personal and national solutions.

The authors bring deep expertise to the problem of medical debt. **Jerry Ashton** has more than 40 years of experience in the credit and collections industry. **Robert Goff** recently retired from 40 years in healthcare management. **Craig Antico** has 30 years in collections, debt buying, outsourcing, and consulting.

This trio together created RIP Medical Debt. Jerry is the founder and Executive Director. Craig is the founder and Operations Director. Robert is RIP's founding board member.

Offering 40 years in journalism, I serve as the book's editor and publisher at my Hoku House. For friend Jerry, I published the 2016 book he wrote with Robert Goff — *The Patient, The Doctor and The Bill Collector: A Medical Debt Survival Guide*. That book led to RIP appearing on the HBO series, "Last Week Tonight with John Oliver." The rest is history, part of which is told in these pages.

When "Obamacare" survived a Senate vote, I suggested updating the book. Jerry wanted to write a new, more current book. Robert wanted to speak more openly than he could when still a healthcare administrator. Craig felt a passion to express his own insights. So, here we are. *End Medical Debt* is the fruit of our collaboration.

You need to know only two more things.

First, each author agreed to write his chapters without seeing the others' work, waiting to read the full book until the layout was done. The views of each author are his own. Balancing their distinct voices has been my distinct pleasure as editor.

Second, Hoku House pays the authors *85 percent* of all the book revenues (opposite of most book deals where authors get a pittance). **The authors donate ALL of their royalties to forgive medical debt!** Each book sold may abolish $500 in unpayable medical bills.

— JF

END MEDICAL DEBT

*Debt, n. An ingenious substitute
for the chain and whip of the slavedriver.*
— AMBROSE BIERCE

CHAPTER 1

Seeing Through the Tears

Jerry Ashton

One of the most difficult tasks we at RIP Medical Debt face on a daily basis is reading entreaty emails from people around the country who beg us to relieve their medical debt burdens.

Here's a sampling of the heart-moving postings at our website:

"I'd appreciate it if you would help me pay my medical bills. I am unemployed at this time. Between the student loan and medical bills, I cannot make it anymore."

"I need help! I am $30,000 in debt and having a hard time keeping up with payments. They keep calling me to ask for the money."

"It's hard to sleep now, hard to find some emotionally peace of mind. I owe so much. I'm just tired of being harassed, but no one listens to me."

"I feel like I am drowning. I am trying to clean up my credit, and all I have is medical debt. My health is not cooperating, but I do not want to incur more bills. I honestly do not know what else to do."

"Two major surgeries in past 12 months. Cannot pay the copay. Have been denied disability twice. Lost my job. Losing my insurance next month. Don't know what to do."

"I managed to make monthly payments and pay some of the doctors in full, but my well is empty, and so is my stomach. I have $2 in my bank account until my Social Security check is deposited. It's getting a bit difficult going on like this."

"My husband was diagnosed with cancer, and he is buried in medical debt since then with no relief in sight."

"My wife and I have both have taken on extra work outside our full-time jobs, just to try to pay down the debt. At the beginning of the year, we drew up a budget to again try and tackle this debt. We realized the only hope was to go bankrupt. It has become impossible. I'm feeling more and more depressed."

"My husband was laid off last year and has not found another job. His unemployment runs out next month.... I got a medical bill for a one-night hospital stay. We have gone through our savings, 401(k) and an inheritance, but I'm determined not to let our credit be destroyed. I called the hospital and went on a five-year payment plan at $100 a month. That may not seem like much, but I'm the one who deals with all the finances, and I'm breaking down in tears on a daily basis from dealing with all of this."

The tears of such suffering people evoke our own. You may cry because of their severe financial straits. I personally weep because the medical debt forgiveness charity I helped start still lacks sufficient means to help all who desperately need debt relief.

Medical Debt: The Hidden Problem

Our nation fervently debates the nature and future of the health care system. Whether one favors or opposes the Affordable Care Act (Obamacare), concerned people across the political spectrum agree something must be done about the growing numbers of Americans who are uninsured or underinsured. Health coverage is the topic. The national conversation has overlooked medical debt.

Let's start with seven evidence-based (ergo, indisputable) facts, not political opinions, concerning the impact of unpaid medical debt on individuals, families, communities, and society itself.

NationalBankruptcy.com reports that:

1. The United States spends more per capita (per person) on health care than any other country on earth.

2. About 1 in 10 adults delay medical care because of its cost.

3. An unexpected $500 medical bill is too much for many people to pay, let alone pay in a timely manner.

4. One in five, or 20 percent, of all working-age Americans with health insurance have trouble paying their medical bills.

5. More than 60 percent of insured Americans with medical bills will deplete most or all of their savings to pay these bills.

6. About 60 percent of the people with problems paying medical bills were contacted by a collection agency in the past year.

7. Health insurance annually has become less affordable since 2015, when the Affordable Care Act went into effect.

Based on our research at RIP, I'll add that 43 million Americans now have about $75 billion in past-due medical debt on their credit reports. We estimate the total of reported and unreported unpaid medical debt in America at about *$1 trillion over ten years.*

How can this be happening in one of the world's most robust economies? Well, a major reason is that our economy values profits. Whether that's good or bad, it's a fact. You may or may not be a fan of "capitalism," but it drives our economic system.

As a result, while we do not burden our population with high taxes for health care like so-called

> Our national conversation has overlooked medical debt.

"socialist" nations, dollars saved in taxes instead are siphoned off by insurance premiums, copays, out-of-pocket medical expenses, and insurance policies that do not cover us fully or not at all (if we have insurance), plus deductibles that can run into thousands annually.

Everybody up and down this chain of pain profits from medical care, even my own industry of debt buyers and collection agencies. Everybody profits, but not the patient.

Our medical care profit system may not be so bad if we're getting our money's worth. Are we? In the September 2018 issue of Managed Care, Joseph Burns challenged Americans, saying, "Hey, big spender! Why does your quality lag so far behind other countries?"

The USA in 2016 spent $10,348 per capita on health care, almost double the average ($5,198) from 11 comparable nations. Citing statistics showing these other countries do much better in a number of health categories, he asked, how do we solve our gap in care?

Adding injury to insult, Americans do not really live longer than citizens in countries with universal healthcare. Economics professor John Komlos wrote in a "PBS News Hour" column that in 2015, the average life expectancy in the United States was 79.3 years, less than in Canada at 82.2 years. Canadian babies can expect to live three years longer than babies born south of the 49th parallel.

How much would it be worth to you if you could live three years longer? Who cares what you label a healthcare system if it delivers a better product? Forget "alternative facts." Look at the hard evidence of costs and inefficiencies in the U.S. healthcare system.

The Five Stages of Healthcare Grief

In my mind, facing the enormity of the personal and national financial costs of the broken U.S. healthcare system is like facing the five stages of grief identified by Dr. Elisabeth Kubler-Ross: *Denial, anger, bargaining, depression;* and *acceptance.*

Kubler-Ross dealt with *sanely* grieving the death of a loved one. Does that apply? We see enough of healthcare in nations that have mandated free or universal coverage that we may sanely feel grief for what we do not have here in our country. In real ways, we Americans turn out to be the healthcare have-nots.

The USA stands alone among 33 highly developed countries by not having universal healthcare coverage. The USA ranks among such poor nations as Afghanistan, Cambodia, Chad, Gambia, Haiti, Iraq, and Zimbabwe, which also do not offer free medical care or universal healthcare. This is not a good thing, in my eyes.

> **Americans turn out to be the healthcare have-nots.**

Let's now explore the analogy of Kubler-Ross' five stages of grief. Seeing through our tears may be a life-affirming resolution for going forward as a much more complete person and healthy nation.

Denial: Think about the many plays on that word — denial. Ever had a claim denied? Ever watch a politician deny any culpability for keeping in place an economically crippling healthcare system? Ever looked at a hospital bill and exclaimed, "This can't be true!"

"Denial helps us to pace our feelings of grief," says Grief.com, "There is a grace in denial. [Denial] is nature's way of letting in only as much as we can handle." Denial is the first step in unwittingly beginning the healing process. "As you proceed, all the feelings you were denying begin to surface."

Some deny the brokenness of our current system, or the value of universal healthcare, by claiming our profit-centered system yields the best health care in the world. Or if our care isn't the best, at least we don't have to wait in line to get it. Factually, that's not so.

> **Among eleven major nations, U.S. healthcare ranks last.**

The U.S. does not have the best healthcare system on earth. In fact, The Commonwealth Fund rates the USA worst among 11 high-income nations. As reported by Newsweek on July 14, 2017, we rank last or close to last in access, administrative efficiency, equity, and care outcomes.

"The U.S. rated especially poor in equality of coverage," stated Newsweek. The magazine reported that 44 percent of low-income Americans have trouble gaining access to coverage compared with 26 percent of high-income Americans. The numbers for the UK are 7 percent and 4 percent, respectively. The UK's National Health Service was deemed the world's best healthcare system, actually, just as it was in 2014. In contrast to the USA over the past decade, the report said, "The UK saw a larger decline in mortality amenable to health care than the other countries studied."

Why deny denial? Feel grief for what we do not have.

Anger: The shift from tears to anger was exemplified in 2017 by late-night talk show host Jimmy Kimmel when he pilloried Rep. Bill Cassidy (R-LA), who'd vowed to replace the ACA with a law that passed the "Jimmy Kimmel test."

"I don't know what happened to Bill Cassidy," Kimmel told his live audience. "He said he wants coverage for all, no discrimination based on preexisting conditions, lower premiums for middle-class families, and no lifetime caps." Kimmel paused. "Guess what? The new [healthcare] bill does none of these things."

At the time, Republican town halls nationwide erupted in voter cries for "repeal and replace," but the ACA replacement bill did not pass, thanks to one "no" vote by the late Sen. John McCain.

Psychologist Jeremy Dean asserts that an upside to anger may be gaining attention and raising awareness. We simply need to do a better job of harnessing anger for constructive purposes as we engage in the urgent national debate over healthcare.

Bargaining: In the case of healthcare, is this a bargain with the devil? Threatening a government shutdown in early 2018, the GOP leveraged the Children's Health Insurance Program (CHIP), which provides low-cost coverage to children in families earning too much to qualify for Medicaid but not enough to buy private insurance. In some states, CHIP covers pregnant women, too. For me, such "chips on the table" for politicians are a losing game for the public. Over the years, many a "grand bargain" has been cobbled together only to fail. Propositions ardently loved and championed by one side were automatically hated and reviled by the other.

Can such conflict qualify as bargaining? Political bargains require members of the opposition to be consulted and worked with openly. Not in today's Congress! The gulf widens. Positions solidify.

Depression: The most obvious definition is that people enter a really unhappy mental state. As Grief.com declares, "Empty feelings present themselves, and grief enters into our lives on a deeper level, deeper than we ever imagined." While depression from grief feels as if it will last forever, such depression is not a sign of mental illness. It's an "appropriate response to a great loss."

I can and do feel the depression and the hopelessness out there. Here are a few depressing emails we get at RIP Medical Debt:

"I had a heart attack and two cardiac procedures in the last year. My husband had a heart attack two years before."

"I've had cancer for three years. Unpaid bills are in collections."

"I'm on a fixed income, struggling to pay my past-due bills."

"I have no money to my name, and I fear becoming homeless. I'm not sure where else to turn."

Acceptance: People stumble with this word. For some, it implies passive surrender to unthinkable brutality. For others, it symbolizes giving permission to hostile forces to do as they will, or accepting that we no longer have a choice. I subscribe to the Reinhold Niebuhr approach, as adapted into the Serenity Prayer: "God, grant me the serenity to accept the things I cannot change, the courage to change the things I can, and the wisdom to know the difference."

In the case of our healthcare system, as I see it, acceptance means coming to realize, "It is what it is." I accept that fuming and raging about it draws attention, but it changes little or nothing. I accept that bargaining does not produce a satisfying resolution. I accept that depression is an emotional trap ensuring no energy is left to search for viable solutions, let alone try to apply them.

Let's say we face the facts as we understand them and accept the things apparently beyond our ability to change. The next requisite step is to find the courage to change those things we can. This book cannot alter the facts, but we can help you understand the situation and educate you on those things that can be changed.

With a prayer for the wisdom to know the difference between the possible and impossible, we can find serenity by seeing clearly what can be changed and what may never change. We then can put our wisdom and knowledge to work. That's our goal here.

Awareness, Compassion, Education, Action

Perhaps the first time you heard about medical debt was in 2016, when HBO's "Last Week Tonight with John Oliver" did a segment on debt buyers. To show how ridiculously easy it is to buy and collect old debt, LWT spent $60,000 to buy a "portfolio" of unpaid medical billing accounts with a face value of almost $15 million.

Rather than collect on that debt, John Oliver in the live studio pushed a big red button to signal donating it all to RIP Medical Debt, our startup charity, which then forgave the debts of nearly 9,000 people in Texas — the largest giveaway in American TV history. His viewers were enthralled. We were thrilled.

Overnight, RIP became a "hot" news story. Overnight, donations began flowing in (plus debt relief pleas). In the prior two years since Craig Antico, Robert Goff and I launched RIP, we'd barely brought in $50,000. That was eclipsed in one day. RIP can buy debt at about a penny on the dollar, so the big surge let us forgive more millions in medical debt. We call this impact "The John Oliver Effect."

RIP began receiving proposals for debt forgiveness campaigns by community groups, trade unions, churches, veterans, high school students, and others As a result of such activity, by the end of 2018, RIP will have abolished close to $1 billion in medical debt!

> Awareness of medical debt is only the first step to a cure.

Awareness: After all this exposure, we realized public awareness is only a first step toward curing our national scourge of medical debt. It's not enough. At least three more steps are needed.

Compassion: We cannot control anyone's willingness to care, but compassion is crucial in gaining public support to abolish medical debt. The dictionary defines compassion as "sympathetic pity and concern for the sufferings or misfortune of others." The John Oliver piece did not resonate with all TV viewers, but more than enough responded compassionately to make a big difference.

This book aims to make you aware about how and why medical debt exists. If you resonate with the pain of the unfortunate people who suffer from often-involuntary medical debt due to an illness or accident, we will give you grist for your compassion mill.

We hope that feeling empathy leads you to take the next step toward actually solving the social problem of medical debt.

Education: Perhaps you seek ways to resolve your own medical debt? Perhaps you seek to end what many see as a national disgrace? We learned that John Oliver's viewers wanted to educate themselves about medical debt and RIP's work. How do we know? Our website crashed from all the traffic. People wanted to know more.

Action: We believe that awareness, compassion and education lead to the fourth necessary step — action! Now that you've become aware medical debt is a huge problem in America, now that you've been touched by others' tears and troubles, now that you've begun educating yourself by reading this book, you may more clearly know what cannot be changed, and what can be changed. We will ask you to act upon whatever wisdom you gather.

Based on our work at RIP, here is how it may be for you:

Awareness	=	OMIGOD!
Compassion	=	That's not right!
Education	=	I need to know more.
Action	=	I must do something about it!

People respond strongly to hope and silver linings if there's proof. For evidence, let me leave you with two more emails:

> "When I think of all the challenging issues facing us, it's easy to feel helpless. However, when I found out about RIP Medical Debt (from John Oliver), the world seemed to brighten. You have shown us that great ideas and hard work can really make a big difference. I know not everyone will get one of your [yellow] debt forgiveness letters in the mail, but

Awaken your heart, educate your mind and choose to act.

your organization is still young. I'll spread the word on social media and say that making a donation in honor of somebody is a great and noble gift. I'd also love to be a volunteer."

Another posting on our website truly made our day:

"I just saw a story about you on 'NBC Nightly News,' and I must admit I am in the same exact boat as you once were in. I'm a debt collections analyst, and today I almost cried while on the phone with a person I called to ask for a payment that I know he just can't pay. He only collects Social Security checks at age 71, yet he has well over $10,000 in medical debt. I literally wanted to transport through the phone and give him a hug to tell him it will be okay. So, I have to say the news segment inspires me, and it gives me hope to see that people are helping, that people out there have a good heart."

In future, the only tears we want to see through are tears of joy. We hope you take action, whatever your favorite solution, and work with others to end medical debt in America — for good!

The first wealth is health.

— Ralph Waldo Emerson

CHAPTER 2

Medical Debt Is the Enemy of Everyone

Robert Goff

Medical debt is the enemy of the patient as well as the physician, the hospital, the community, the state, and the nation.

When we think about the debts of others, we generally think of such debts as their responsibility. If they are unable to pay that debt, it's *their* problem. (We make it a *You* problem, not a *Me* problem) After all, society tells us, isn't a problem with personal debt a direct consequence of bad decision-making, bad personal financial habits, profligate spending, or living beyond one's means?

We may think the consequences of debt are rightly visited on a person. Whatever the impact — canceled credit cards, low credit, wage garnishment — it's on them. Personal responsibility.

Is this true? In the big picture, we individuals and society both bear the costs and burdens of our personal "bad debt."

For any individuals who fall into arrears in their payments, who cannot pay their past financial obligations, unpaid debt means their ability to purchase goods and services is curtailed or perhaps ended. If new credit is not extended, the person must live on cash.

For any business, debt that cannot be paid by the customer who created it becomes a cost to the enterprise that extended credit. The business may recoup a loss by raising prices for products or services. The business may stop a loss by not providing goods or services to a debtor, which disciplines those failing to pay their bills.

In such cases, the consequences of unpaid personal debt fall on the debtor *and* on the creditor, usually ending there.

This does not apply to medical debt. *Personal debt created by an inability to pay for necessary medical services is called medical debt.* The consequences of medical debt extend beyond individuals and service providers. Medical debt ripples outward, adversely affecting physicians, hospitals, communities, the nation, perhaps requiring government intervention, which impacts the taxpayer — you.

The Debt Daisy Chain

Medical debt is not like a debt incurred by buying a big screen TV one cannot afford. It should not be treated the same way.

Medical debt is largely the result of an unplanned, involuntary event, often an illness or accident. It is not a choice. Illness is never chosen. Sure, certain lifestyle choices, personal habits and emotional habits can lessen chances for good health. Smoking, drinking, illicit drugs, unhealthy foods, or other risky behaviors are private choices. However, no one consciously volunteers to be ill. No one volunteers for a personal injury accident, either. Medical debt is not about living beyond one's means. Medical debt is about staying alive.

If people are unable to take personal financial responsibility for the economic results of medical efforts to restore (or try to restore) them to good health, medical debt is incurred. Having medical debt impacts access to medical services, when the only care available is a hospital emergency room — the care location of last resort. An ER is the most costly and least appropriate for non-urgent care.

Unlike other sellers of goods or services, medical providers do not cut off a debtor from all care. Medical debt will impact the care a debtor receives, and where, but medical services are to be available in some form. Physicians take an oath: Do no harm. Healers cannot ethically let people suffer.

> For individuals, medical debt is a barrier to good health.

Among all of the medical care providers, the physicians and the hospitals bear the most economic burden from medical debt. Their patients' unpaid bills impact the rest of the healthcare system.

Unlike commercial enterprises, hospitals and physicians do not routinely recover losses by increasing prices for those patients who *can* pay their bills. In today's U.S. economic environment of private health insurance and government health insurance, the majority of payment rates are controlled by contracts or regulations.

Medicare and Medicaid reimbursements to medical providers, are based on formulas tied to the costs of delivering care, not the true business costs for delivering that care. Insurance plans pay the lowest rates possible, based on competitive fiscal factors. Physicians, hospitals and other care providers cannot simply increase their fees to cover their accumulating losses from unpaid medical debts.

For individuals, medical debt is a barrier to good health. Poor health means a loss of job productivity, maybe less income, which lessens contributions to family wellbeing, reducing contributions to the economics of society through employment taxes.

For medical providers like hospitals, the unpaid costs of medical care can reduce their financial viability. Some seek taxpayer support through government programs to stay viable. Any taxpayer support translates into higher taxes for a locality or state. Businesses tend to avoid expanding or relocating in high-tax areas. Higher local taxes reduce an area's desirability for future economic growth. A higher proportion of medical indigents in a community reduces the area's desirability as a place where physicians wish to practice. Less health care cuts a community's desirability for workers, and for business, so there are fewer jobs, further depressing the local economy.

Back to individuals, medical debt — and a fear of incurring more medical debt— drives the calculation of care vs. cost. When medical costs outstrip an individual's and family's economic ability to pay, the resulting medical debt gets between a patient and vital medical care as needed. "Should I go to the doctor?" becomes "Can I afford to see the doctor?" "Should I fill this prescription?" becomes, "Can I afford to fill it?" Too often, cost wins over care.

Consider the full human costs in desperate situations. In Boston on July 4, 2018, UPI reported, a woman's leg was caught between a subway car and the platform, ripping her flesh to the bone. Crying in agony, she pleaded with her rescuers not to call an ambulance. "It's $3,000," she wailed. "I can't afford that!"

Consider the interconnected social daisy chain of medical debt. What impacts one impacts all.

Gaps in Medical Care

When medical insurance is lacking, or has gaps in coverage that limit protection against dire financial hardship, economics weigh heavily on a personal decision whether or not to seek medical care. If care is sought, insurance coverage, or its lack, affects the decision to follow treatment plans or to fill prescriptions.

Health insurance gaps, such as ever-higher deductibles, coupled with the increasingly byzantine rules for insurance coverage, impact those struggling with health decisions. One in three Americans delay seeking medical care for themselves or family members due to the cost of medical care, according to a 2014 Gallup poll reported in The Daily Caller. That percentage has risen since 2010 enactment of the Affordable Care Act (ACA). The sad increase in delayed treatment primarily can be attributed to the raising of insurance deductibles. *Higher deductibles tend to add to medical debt.*

Failures to follow recommended treatments, such as not taking prescriptions, is not solely due to costs. A 2015 National Center for Health Statistics study found only eight percent of Americans don't take their medicines as prescribed because they cannot afford them. Nearly 20 percent of all prescriptions never get filled.

Delayed or missed care can raise costs by increasing illness. When put-off care at last is sought, the medical costs are inevitably higher, the outcomes predictably poorer. The economic impacts of more extensive and expensive care add to medical debt burdens on everyone.

The poor or near-poor are not the only ones who delay care due to cost concerns. Gallup reported that following the first year of the start for the Affordable Care Act, aka "Obamacare," about 38 percent of middle-class people delayed medical care due to cost, up 33 percent over the prior year. Gallup surveyed households with annual incomes between $30,000 and $75,000. Among households earning above $75,000 annually, about 28 percent told Gallup they delayed care, more than the 17 percent in 2013. So, roughly a third of all "affluent" Americans delay care regardless of the costs to themselves or society.

Economic impacts continue once treatment starts. The Cancer Support Center, reports USA Today, found more than 20 percent of cancer patients skipped recommended treatments, fearing high out-of-pocket costs. Almost 50 percent said their costs were higher than expected. Their cost concerns delayed screening tests, which ment delayed treatment. Such non-compliance from cost concerns reduces the effectiveness of treatment. In cancer care, early detection and treatment yields the best outcomes. Fear of medical debt caused later disease discovery, later treatment, and less favorable outcomes. We face gaps in care.

Medical Debt Poverty Trap

For individuals, the ultimate economic consequence of medical debt could be impoverishment. After personal and family resources are exhausted, if impoverished, they are eligible for publicly funded medical insurance, like Medicaid, or maybe charity assistance.

Medicaid benefits tends to be as complete as commercial health insurance coverage, often without deductibles. Medicaid limits the choice of providers, and it carries negative social connotations. Still, the coverage is often better than employer-provided insurance. To receive Medicaid, though, you do have to live in poverty.

Comprehensive insurance with high deductibles contributes to delayed care from money worries — increasing illness and depleting financial resources, making one eligible for Medicaid.

Medicaid or charity assistance is not an escape. Such help comes to the rescue only after the patient or the family has "spent down," depleting their financial reserves, perhaps due to limited or absent insurance coverage. *Seems to me bitterly ironic that families must be economically destroyed before they are eligible for the care that would have avoided the harm in the first place.* Medical indigence can trap individuals and families into actual poverty.

Medicaid or charity care is not an escape for patients.

The hard truth is that access to medical charity comes only after a patient or family is deemed insolvent or in poverty, too often from medical debt. Most charities, unlike Medicaid, do not cover any medical debts accumulated prior to entering their programs.

Costly care depletes family resources, which extends out into the community of taxpayers. The involuntary physical burden of an illness or accident stays with the individual and family, yet the wider economic costs are borne by the entire community and the nation as a whole. Medical debt affects the economic ecosystem.

Taxes fund state and federal government healthcare programs. The ACA, Obamacare, dramatically increased the number of people eligible for Medicaid on a state-by-state basis, including those near the poverty line and below it. In many states, legislatures provided hospitals with funds for the indigent. Same as with Medicaid, state hospital support programs are financed by taxpayers.

When hospitals provide charity care, under current rules, costs may be offset by higher fees to their patients' insurance companies. Charity care is offset by higher premiums paid by those who are not charity cases. Where a hospital cannot pass on its charity costs, when Medicaid payments are insufficient, additional government financial assistance may be needed to keep the hospital's doors open. As a vital community resource and major employer in a community, hospitals too often must rely on taxpayer-financed rescues.

Public resentment at growing tax burdens has severely restrained Medicaid reimbursements. This means Medicaid is not an attractive payment source for providers, so only a fraction of any local medical community participates in the program. Inadequate reimbursement for indigent care by Medicaid means patients often are limited to public or charity clinics or episodic emergency room care. A stable physician-patient relationship or "continuum of care" is lost.

Low Medicaid reimbursements in some places attract only care providers with less-desirable training or talent, not those able to earn a living with payments from insurance or affluent patients.

Poorer care for poorer people costs all the taxpayers more. The medical-gap trap impacts everyone in American society.

Insurance Is No Protection

People who have health insurance are wise not to feel too secure in their coverage. Insured people are at risk of medical debt.

Employers mitigate their health insurance premium increases by decreasing coverage and increasing employee deductibles (amounts employees pay out-of-pocket before insurance kicks in).

> Employers mitigate premium increases by decreasing coverage and increasing employee deductibles.

CBS News "Money Watch" reported deductibles had surged 67 percent since 2010, yet workers' earnings increased only 10 percent. By 2016, found CBS, about 51 percent of all workers with insurance had deductibles greater than $1,000. Deductibles considerably higher than $1,000 are increasingly common.

At the same time, employers pass along to employees more of their costs for higher insurance premiums. From 2010 to 2016, finds a Kaiser Family Foundation study of health benefits, workers' contribution to health premiums increased 78 percent. Still, worker earnings rose only 10 percent, a net loss for them.

A separate 2015 Kaiser Family Foundation study found that:

- 62 percent of those stressed by medical bills have insurance.
- 75 percent of those insured say insurance copays, deductibles, or coinsurance are more than they can afford.
- 46 percent of insured workers face annual deductibles of $1,000 or more for single coverage (up from 41 percent in 2014).
- 39 percent of large firms that offer employee health insurance have plans with deductibles of $1,000 or more.
- 20 percent of those with health insurance say paying medical bills has caused serious financial disruption in their lives.
- 11 percent of insured workers end up seeking charity aid.

Simply put, higher health costs are eating more of workers' pay, leaving them exposed to more costs and more medical debt.

Most health insurance is tied to employment. What can keep any working person awake at night is the reality that the coverage he or she has could disappear in the morning with a pink slip. The loss of employment, like from an accident or illness, can quickly move a middle-income family into medically induced poverty.

That's not what's supposed to happen.

COBRA Costs

In the event of job loss, federal law protects workers' ability to keep employer-sponsored health insurance. Called COBRA (from the Consolidated Omnibus Budget Reconciliation Act), such health care coverage costs more than when employed.

Under COBRA, a former employee may pay up to 102 percent of a former employer's own insurance premium. If an injury causes disability, COBRA coverage can be extended, but at a higher cost — up to 150 percent of that employer's whole premium.

The average annual premium for employer-provided coverage in 2017 was $18,764, according to the National Conference of State Legislators. Faced with the loss of income from lost employment, who can sustain the added pressures on the budget from COBRA? Adding to the disaster, even if you can afford COBRA, it's limited to 18 months while job hunting. After that, too bad, so sad. You're on your own. Try to find coverage you can afford.

The designers of COBRA saw coverage as a temporary stop-gap as workers find other jobs with health insurance. No consideration was given to the fact an illness or accident leading to unemployment may preclude re-employment. COBRA mandates the availability of coverage, not affordability, and this assumes a new job has health insurance. Unreal. The Kaiser Family Foundation in 2016 reported only 55 percent of all U.S. employers offer health benefits. The other 45 percent? Voila! New candidates for Medicaid.

Taking Unfair Advantage

Employees paying high payroll deductions for health coverage often share a false sense of security.

After the deductible, they think, the insurance is there to protect my financial wellbeing. Not so.

All coverage has "rules" limiting protections. Intended to keep down insurance premiums, the rules may come as a shock to workers when reality hits: They need coverage for an illness or injury.

Many insurance plans refuse to pay for care, even if medically necessary, when it falls outside their own self-dictated restrictions. Emergencies may not be covered if they require pre-authorization. Out-of-network service providers may not be covered except in proven life-threatening emergencies.

Insurance policy rules may stop an insurer from accepting fiscal responsibility for paying your medical bill.

Much to our detriment, we Americans seldom invest time to understand the limitations of our insurance coverage, the nuances. If a family member or ourselves gets ill or injured, feeling urgency, we may get care without realizing the financial consequences.

Unethical care providers may exploit ignorance of plan coverage. They'll misrepresent participation in any plan to "capture" a patient and the associated revenue.

> We seldom invest time to understand the limitations of our insurance coverage.

Phrases like "participating" or "will bill insurance" or "will take insurance" may be reassuring to the patient, but none of these terms guarantee what the patient thinks they mean.

A confident patient who receives care may get a nasty and costly shock. When their insurance company unexpectedly denies a bill, the patient finds a physician or clinic is not covered by the insurers' contract. Patients suddenly find the bill is their own responsibility. Patients must fight hard for any insurance coverage.

Some patients find themselves on the short end if the physician cuts a deal to accept whatever the insurance pays. No mention may be made of others in a procedure who are not covered. The patient gets a nasty and costly shock. The New York Times in 2014 told of a patient getting a $117,000 bill from an assistant surgeon who was not covered by the patient's plan.

Aetna, the health insurance company, has taken an aggressive stance against enticing patients into financial traps. In New York, they filed a lawsuit against two doctors, in-network Dr. Ramin Rak and out-of-network Dr. Shuriz Hishmeh. Dr. Rak used Dr. Hishmeh as his co-surgeon on procedures. Dr. Rak got $183,294 in-network. Dr. Hishmeh got more than $1.1 million out-of-network. Crain's New York Business reported the patient was liable for all costs for out-of-network surgery above Aetna's allowable rates.

Even if the insurance steps up to protect patients by paying the bills, the cost of financial abuse by out-of-network billing inevitably results in higher health insurance premiums for all.

Some physicians take unfair advantage of unwary patients by providing services in settings that are not covered. A physician may participate in a patient's health plan, for example, but influences a patient to do a procedure at an ambulatory surgery center where the physician has an ownership stake. The non-participating center, unfettered by contract limits, may not hesitate to send a medical bill, a large one. If the bill is not paid, it's medical debt.

> **Patients may be liable for all out-of-network care charges.**

Medical costs can be tricky. A non-contracted or out-of-network private ambulatory surgery center in New York used a contracted, participating doctor for a medical procedure, and the center billed a patient $42,000. Insurance would have paid the participating center about $3,000, and the patient's in-network cost would have been just $1,000. This "double jeopardy" meant that the physician was paid for professional services and then paid again separately as an owner of the ambulatory surgery center, enjoying a portion of all the profits earned out-of-network.

For unwary patients "captured" by non-participating providers, the economic exposures can be tremendous. The impacts include a higher deductible, higher cost-sharing, and being held responsible for the total bill, the totally outrageous bill.

Fiscal Risks of Hospitalization

Hospitalized patients are among those most victimized by out-of-network situations. The breach may be aided and abetted by the very hospital where they sought professional quality care.

If admitted to a hospital, you are dependent on the institution's care structure. You are reduced to an account number, occupying a bed, incurring charges. During your hospital stay, you are subject to a fees structure that may put your economic health at risk. Your body may recover, but your finances may not.

Few people realize that hospitals do not control the health plan participation of physicians granted privileges to use the hospital for admitting and treating patients. This applies to most physicians in community hospitals. Even if a hospital hires the physician directly, it may not take steps to assure the new physician employee contracts or participates in the same health plans as the hospital.

Without your knowing, one or more of your hospital caregivers may not be covered under your plan, such as a physician consulted on your case. The New Jersey Record reported an egregious example at a New Jersey hospital where a patient was billed $56,980 for a 25-minute bedside consultation by a non-participating physician.

Some hospitals make it worse by contracting exclusively with certain physician groups for staffing, but then do not require these groups to participate in the hospitals' health plans.

For example, hospitals often contract with physician groups to provide anesthesia services or to staff the emergency department. These groups agree to provide 24/7 staffing in return for exclusive rights to provide those services. However, the hospital may place no requirements on them to participate with set health plans, claiming participation is an independent business decision of that group.

Some hospitals grant groups sole monopolies over essential care services, and monopolies tend to price monopolistically. Hospital services often granted to monopolies include radiology, pathology, anesthesiology, cardio EKG, and ER department physicians.

CNBC in 2016 reported that out-of-network emergency room doctors, on average, were paid 2.7 times more than in-network ER doctors were paid for doing the same exact services.

Health plans must pay a non-participating physician for care in a life-or-limb emergency visit. Few patients question the insurance participation of the anesthesiologist or radiologist, rarely in elective admissions. If a hospital participates with my insurance, then all the physicians there must participate, too, yes? Not necessarily.

Hospitals and physicians are consolidating into "systems" with the avowed benefit that care is coordinated by providers who all are part of one organization. However, a 2014 Los Angeles Times article confirmed that "in system" may not mean "in network." To cite an extreme example, an out-of-network California pathologist charged $81,000 for a tissue exam while Medicare pays only $128.

The Guardian in 2018 told a compelling story about the birth of three sons to Stella Apo Osae-Cwum, insured, who was driven near to bankruptcy by the out-of-network physician charges at an in-network hospital. She and her husband did it all by the book, used an in-network hospital and obstetrician. When her triplets were born prematurely, a bill came. The hospital's out-of-network neonatologist charged $877,000. Her employer-provided insurance covered most of the bill, but she was responsible for $51,000.

The financial risks to any patient while a "captive" of the hospital can be financially stressful, to put it mildly.

The Costs of 'Free' Hospital Care

Some people go to the hospital without paying. Is their care truly free? According to the American Hospital Association, community hospitals' uncompensated care — including free, discounted, and unpaid care — increased from $35.7 billion in 2015 to $38.3 billion in 2016. The AHA "Uncompensated Care Fact Sheet" reports such care represents 6.2 percent of annual hospital expenses.

Hospitals recover lost revenues with higher charges to paying patients, higher charges to health insurers (who increase insurance premiums), and with government assistance using our taxes.

Medicare and commercial insurance companies largely restrain "cost-shifting" — raising prices on other customers to cover shortfalls in payments from those of limited means.

Is this system just? Perhaps. Consider the impacts.

A great oddity in hospital finance is how uninsured individuals are charged. The patients *with* insurance are charged the discounted rates of insurance carriers. Patients *without* insurance fall into the "self-pay" category. They must fund the full costs of their care.

Uninsured patients, those least likely to have the means to pay the cost of their care, are charged the maximum rates set by the hospital. In the hotel business, how many guests pay the "rack rate" or full price for a room?

A hospital's uncompensated care adds to financial pressures on the institution. The facilities most disadvantaged serve areas with weak local economies. Hospitals in poor and near-poor communities provide the most unpaid care. Hospital closures caused by unmanageable financial losses happen most often in less well-off communities and neighborhoods.

> 'Self pay' patients must fund the full cost of their medical care.

The ripples from a hospital closure are less access to care, loss of a positive economic force for jobs, and the community being less desirable, thereby worsening poverty in the community.

Becker's Hospital Review reports 57 hospitals closed from 2010 to 2015, with 21 closing in 2016, and 10 in 2017. All of the acute-care hospitals closing their doors cited financial pressure as a reason, or even *the* reason, for their closure. Medical debt is not the sole source of hospitals' fiscal distress, yet it certainly does contribute mightily. As a last resort to avoid closure, hospitals seek bailouts from states and municipalities. That cost is borne by us taxpayers.

The Impact on Physicians

Physicians in private practice lack the benefits of a local, state or federal governmental program to offset the impact of bad debt. As patients' debts rise, if a physician is unable to absorb the revenue losses, hard choices must be made. Physicians' responses to excessive medical bad debt, even if ethical, often are unpleasant.

Physicians rarely disengage from a patient over a financial issue. By law and custom, they cannot abandon a patient under their care. If this means providing unpaid care until a patient can find another caregiver, or can be referred away, then so be it.

Patients causing unsustainable financial losses for a physician may be discharged from a medical practice. A discharge may be self-imposed by a patient, embarrassed to owe for past care, who quietly stops making or keeping appointments. They exile themselves.

The physician, sensitive to a patient's fiscal hardship, may refer a patient to another medical resource, such as a community health center or public clinic. The continuity of care is lost.

Physicians face a stark financial reality. They must earn enough revenue to sustain themselves and their practice. Bad debt rarely can be replaced by raising rates. Physicians' rates are fixed by insurance and government rules. Time and resources are expended to extend care. Must doctors absorb the loss? Unfortunate yet understandable collection efforts can ruin a physician-patient relationship.

> **Insurance and government rules ensure doctors must absorb unpaid patient bills.**

A primary care physician may refer the patient for specialty care. The patient's stressed finances may prompt skipping care or the prescriptions. A more ill patient returns to primary care, unable to pay bills, or the patient goes to the more costly hospital ER.

Medical debt, ultimately, may prompt physicians to close or relocate their practices out of the communities they serve. They do not abandon a community they love for callous greed, but for self-survival.

Uncollectable patient bills produce an uneven distribution of good physicians in our communities, creating "healthcare deserts." Given a choice, few physicians locate practices in distressed areas, where the need is greatest, unless fulfilling a duty of their medical education.

Some programs forgive physicians' medical school student debt if they agree to practice several years in an underserved community, like working for a clinic or hospital in a rural area. Their service usually is short term unless lasting bonds form within that community.

The institutions supporting temporary local physicians rely on government financing. Such "supported" medical practices add to the ways medical costs and related debt become financial obligations for the whole community of taxpayers.

The structure of medical insurance coverage virtually assures physicians in private practice have unpaid bills. Reliable data for their medical debt is hard to locate because most medical practices use cash-based accounting (recording income when received and expenses when paid). Bad debt is not counted as income or expense, so it's missed. Some studies indicate that bad debt can run between

5.9 percent and 14 percent of any physician's billings. A 2013 Kaiser Family Foundation study found that private office-based physicians provided more than $30 billion in uncompensated care.

If a physician closes an office due to bad debt, the patients suffer disruption of their care, and the community loses a caregiver. The impact spreads outward into society.

The Impact on Patients

The ACA was supposed to solve health care issues by removing financial status as a barrier to obtaining medical care. It didn't work. Medical insecurity continues as Congressional and court activities put the ACA benefits in doubt, such as full coverage for preexisting conditions, for preventive care without copays or deductibles..

> **ACA theory and ACA reality do not match.**

The ACA's failure to cut the costs of delivering health services contributes to the upward spiral of premiums, which translates into higher payroll dedications or increased deductibles. More than ever now, ACA theory and reality do not match.

If health is restored and people can return to the workforce with paid insurance, they remain liable for *all accumulated prior debt*. To pay off old bills, they often skip or skimp on needed medication and follow-up care. This is especially true (and most troubling) for those with chronic diseases, like diabetes, where skipping treatment can rapidly deteriorate health, resulting in far higher care bills.

Not filling a prescription can be costly and deadly. ProMed.gov compared patients who follow instructions to those who don't take medications as intended, including for financial reasons. They risk hospitalization, re-hospitalization and premature death 5.4 times higher in cases of hypertension, 2.8 times higher with dyslipidemia, and 1.5 times higher in cases of heart disease.

"Putting it off" is no solution. Studies report people who delay or forego care are less likely to report "very good" or "excellent" health. They have lower quality-of-life scores compared to those who do not delay necessary medical care.

According to a 2013 University of Chicago/AP national survey "Privately Insured in America: Opinions on Health Care Costs and Coverage," among adults from ages 18 to 64 with private insurance, 19 percent not visit the doctor when sick, and 18 percent go without preventive or recommended care.

An unfortunate impact of all the byzantine rules for coverage is patients' confusion on benefits and concern for costs, which keeps them from early detection and treatment of their ailments.

A short-term savings by skipping a cancer screening may yield a later identification of more advanced cancer. It's a classic scenario of "pay me now or pay me later." If cancer is identified too late for successful treatment, patients may pay with their lives.

Being wise enough to seek medical treatment, but not being able to pay the medical bills, creates its own set of challenges.

That 2015 Kaiser Family Foundation study found nationwide averages for how people handle high costs for medical care:

- 77 percent cut spending for household purchases or vacations.
- 63 percent use up most or all of their savings.
- 42 percent take an extra job or work more hours.
- 38 percent increase their credit card debt or max out the cards.
- 37 percent borrow money from family or friends.
- 14 percent change their living situations.

Even with insurance, millions of Americans are living only one accident or illness away from potential economic disaster. Could you and your family handle a serious illness or injury?

Medical debt from medical care is the great equalizer. According to Kaiser, about 44 percent of those with employer-provided health insurance shared nearly identical consequences by paying medical bills as the 45 percent paying for their healthcare without insurance. Medical debt is an equal opportunity destroyer.

Collections and Bankruptcy

If people do not pay their medical bills, collections begin!

Aggressively pursued medical debt is destructive to individuals' and families' stability and security. Bill collectors compel debtors to choose between paying rent, food, transportation, childcare, or other overdue bills. To satisfy bill collection demands, those with limited means may be forced to miss a mortgage payment or not put tires on their car. Some may give up on even trying to be a "responsible" person, refusing to answer the phone or open the mail.

Bloomberg News in 2014 ran a story on a William Piorun facing an impossible choice between paying for his mortgage or paying for his medications, which cost $20,000 a month. He had coverage, but his copay was more than $1,000 per month. How does he live?

Urgency increases when any professional bill collector enters the scene. Their aim is singular and purposeful: Collect monies owed to their health-provider clients, regardless of the grim consequences from the life decisions they force patients to make.

Adding more injury, many employers now verify credit reports on prospective employees before hiring them. Any medical debt on a credit report can deter or prevent employment.

Glassdoor in 2018 reported that as many as 60 percent of all employers do credit checks on their job prospects. The presumption is that those under financial stress, or who have difficulty managing personal finances, may be less responsible or more likely to commit white-collar crime, so they are less desirable as employees.

With credit scores integral to hiring decisions, medical debt on a credit report narrows folks' job prospects, hurting their economic recovery and financial stability. Bluntly, medical debt can prevent earning the money to pay the medical debt.

NerdWallet Health in 2013 cited medical debt as the number one cause of bankruptcies in the USA, outpacing credit card debt and unpaid mortgages. Further, NerdWallet indicated that about 56 million adults — 20 percent of the population between the ages of 19 and 64 — struggled with paying care-related bills that year. They have not updated their report, but I believe it's greater today.

> Medical debt can prevent earning money to pay the debt.

Bankruptcy releases debt, but it stays 10 years on a credit report. Credit is denied people, negatively affecting reconstruction of their lives. Forget about a mortgage or a car loan, and that's for starters. Even after all the debt is discharged, enduring punishments from personal bankruptcy are anything but a "clean slate."

If you think the ultimate consequence of unpaid medical bills is bankruptcy, a 2017 story in the Miami New Times reports medical debt in South Florida is the leading cause of homelessness. It beat out mental illness and drug use as the top reasons. Medical debt even beat out job loss as the primary cause of Miami homelessness.

Personal Responsibility

Personal responsibility matters, yet debt from necessary medical care is innately different than debt from living beyond one's means. Survival not vanity is the real cause of medical debt. Whether or not the economic impacts are noticed, medical debt affects us all.

Healthcare is an interconnected system. Medical debt drives up our insurance premiums and deductibles. Medical debt drives up our taxes for Medicare and Medicaid, drives up our taxes for saving local medical institutions. Personal medical debt does not stop with the debtor. Medical debt ultimately gets paid by the taxpayers.

All of us pay for medical debt, if not our own, then the medical debt of others. As rising medical costs outstrip individuals' ability to pay, the impacts go beyond the amount of any medical bill. We may argue about the costs of health care. We may argue about solutions. Debate is good but not enough. *Medical debt is the elephant in the room nobody wants to talk about.* We cannot get around it.

Commercial insurance, Medicare, Medicaid, and charity care promise protection and relief from medical impoverishment. But the social safety net has gaping holes for individuals, and communities pay the price, as does our entire nation. Medical debt is the enemy of everyone. That's not what we expect here in America.

CHAPTER 3

Debt Mountains Cause Healthcare Deserts

Craig Antico

We all bear the costs of medical debt, as Robert says, so why are we ignoring and allowing material hardships from mounting debt to fall upon certain identifiable groups of people? If these people are inordinately burdened by medical debt to the point it negatively affects their psyche, behavior and wellbeing, have we not a collective responsibility to right this wrong?

How does medical debt affect individuals' health and wellbeing? What about such *social determinants* as isolation, income insecurity, transportation insecurity, education level, access to healthcare, and living environment? We're now finding out.

Researchers at the economics and public policy departments of UCLA, UC/Berkeley, University of Chicago, and MIT have released the preliminary finding of an economic impact study to measure the effects of medical debt forgiveness by RIP (see Chapter 8). The findings shed light on how medical debt affects people's wellbeing. We hope these findings influence public policy.

I believe insurmountable "debt mountains" may determine our wellbeing when we behave as if we're living in "healthcare deserts," when we choose not to access needed healthcare, even if available, from fear of the costs and stress resulting from medical debt.

Who all is buried on debt mountain? Those in poverty and with limited public support and resources. Youth in their late twenties. Those with severe diseases (like cancer, mental illness or addiction). Forty million working-class Americans earning an average of $12 an hour with no company-provided health insurance. The veterans denied VA coverage. All are buried on debt mountain.

Hardship, Poverty, Poor Health

What percentage of people do you believe experience poverty, poor health or material hardship each year?

The Centers for Disease Control and Prevention reports only 7.6 percent of people in the USA are admitted to the hospital overnight every year. Such a relatively low usage of the healthcare system contributes to a common misperception that medical debt doesn't affect that many people. Look closer.

According to a three-year study by the Robin Hood Foundation and Columbia University Population Research Center, 63 percent of the residents studied in a community experienced an economic hardship in one year. Specifically, this 63 percent experienced one or more of the defining criteria of being disadvantaged — poverty, hardship and poor health.

Those without savings are the most vulnerable to medical debt.

Poverty: Financial assistance programs pay attention to income levels in determining financial assistance, but "income poverty" can change rapidly by finding a job. A job is not enough. About 69 percent of Americans have less than $1,000 in savings, 49 percent have less than $500, and 34 percent have no savings at all. Those without savings are the most vulnerable to medical debt.

According to a recent Federal Reserve survey, almost 50 percent of all Americans cannot come up with $400 for a sudden bill. They would have to sell off an asset or borrow the funds.

Households with medical debt have 70 percent more credit card debt, plus more debt overall. Sean McElwee in Demos reports that, on average, medically indebted households have $8,762 in credit card debt — compared to households with $5,154 in credit card debt that does not stem from medical bills.

Americans borrow from friends and family to the tune of $55.7 billion per year, Olivia Chow reported in Finder. The disadvantaged rarely have friends and family with that kind of money. They turn to crowdfunding, where 36 percent of all money is raised to pay for medical expenses or its residual debt.

Hardship: The most persistent disadvantage is the inability to pay your bills. For example, the Columbia study found only nine percent of people who entered a year in poverty were in poverty at the end of that year. However, 23 percent of those entering a year in material hardship were still there at the end of the year.

Poor Health: Traditional healthcare interventions account for only 20 percent of a person's health — 80 percent is due to factors like physical environment, health behaviors, and socioeconomic conditions. Changes in income, work or family dynamics are the top three causes of stress, and these drive 75-90 percent of all health care visits and related medical debt. The migration patterns in and out of poverty, hardship and wellbeing need to be better understood by our healthcare system. (RIP uses consumer credit data with social determinant data to assess who qualifies for debt forgiveness.)

Medicaid in the Debt Terrain

Debt mountains are geographically concentrated in states with limited Medicaid coverage. AARP interviewed hundreds of people earning less than $40,000 a year. No one on Medicaid had medical debt. In states that expanded Medicaid coverage under ACA from people earning 100 percent of the poverty level up to 138 percent, we at RIP see fewer requests for debt relief. A gap from 138 to 200 percent of the poverty level still needs to be filled.

We learned by working with the AARP that there is a problem for middle-class spouses who need Medicaid to provide services for a loved one. Once the loved one dies, Medicaid stops paying, and debts mount. It's devastating for me to see a proud, independent person who just lost a spouse to have all their savings clawed back. This debt mountain stays unseen unless the people buried by debt are willing to speak up and be heard.

Uninsured and Underinsured

The Commonwealth Fund considers people "underinsured" if their deductible equals more than 10 percent of their gross income. They comprise most of those who are underinsured. For those who earn less than two times the Federal Poverty Level (FPL) guidelines, if their deductible passes 5 percent of their gross income, they also are called underinsured. The Commonwealth Fund reports that 68 million people in our county are underinsured or uninsured.

Middle Class: The underinsured include people making poor health care choices from being uninformed about medical services, from not understanding what their health insurance actually covers, and the out-of-network providers. They often are in the middle class, earning from 200 percent to 350 percent of the FPL. Despite a good income, they spend at least five percent of their gross income on out-of-pocket medical costs.

> **68 million people in our county are underinsured or uninsured.**

About 20-25 percent of the debt we abolish at RIP is for people in the middle class. They qualify for debt relief by large percentage of their gross income paying for out-of-pocket expenses and debt service. They are more likely to have high out-of-network bills since they want the best care and will "pay" for it, even if the doctor or service is not fully covered under their health plan. That "sensible decision" can be costly,

Working Class: About 44 million people in America are in the "working class," and almost none of them receive health insurance from their employer. Under the ACA, they may purchase health insurance on their own through a government portal.

Youth: The youngest, healthiest workers in their twenties often opt-out of health insurance, or they pick the lowest-premium plan with the highest deductibles. This is why, among all the age groups, 27-year-olds have the most medical debt on their credit reports.

Seniors: Elders often have limited income, and so have high levels of medical debt. As the U.S. population ages, there will be fewer and fewer "free" caregivers. AARP says that in 2018 more than 40 million caregivers will provide at least $470 billion worth of free care-related "hours of service." A 2017 Indiana University study found that tallied $377.6 billion for Medicare and Medicaid, and $410 billion for care donated by individuals, foundations and corporations.

Ailments Atop Debt Mountain

For almost every age and class, mountains of debt keep growing. Those with serious ailments of body and mind too often end up buried on debt mountain. Two examples suggest the scale.

Cancer: As you may know, or someone close to you may know, a cancer diagnosis is devastating. Next, you start getting and paying the bills. A study in the Journal of Clinical Oncology confirmed the bills increase stress and increases early mortality.

More than one-third of the cancer patients with insurance pay more out-of-pocket for treatments than they expected to spend. A Duke University survey found patients in the study were paying an average of 11 percent on out-of-pocket costs for cancer treatment, said lead author Fumiko Chino, M.D, at Duke Health. Patients in the study who reported the most financial distress were spending 30 percent of their household income on health care.

Mental Illness and Addiction: Few health plans cover mental health or addiction treatment services, and these rarely to the extent deemed medically necessary by consumers, caregivers, and doctors. The bills may not show up anywhere in the medical debt statistics. Costs may be paid by friends and family, from savings, credit cards, or by selling a house. Mental health care is a major out-of-network cost because providers want to be paid upfront, or else you or your loved one might not get the help needed.

Kaiser Family Foundation analysis of suicide and intentional injuries,82 percent have more than $1,000 in out-of-pocket expenses (OOP), and 16 percent have OOP expenses over $5,000. The mental health conditions associated with the highest OOP expenses are suicide attempts, psychotic disorders and dementia.

This cost burden is disconcerting. Nearly one-fifth of our total adult population report mental health issues. An insured employee with mental health spending may have out-of-pocket costs passing $5,000, double that of the average health condition. Research by RIP through Definitive Healthcare calculates that out of 35 million inpatient visits to U.S. hospitals, at least 38 percent of them present psychosis as a primary or secondary diagnosis.

DEBT MOUNTAINS CAUSE HEALTHCARE DESERTS

Few are comfortable talking about how mental illness, addiction and medical debt are debilitating America and our families.

Out-of-Network Surprises

America's Health Insurance Plans, the industry trade group, has found that about 12 percent of all U.S. health claims were for care services obtained from out-of-network providers.

AHIP studied 18 billion claims for the 97 most common health services. People who got treatments from doctors and facilities not covered by insurance plans, said AHIP, received bills ranging from 118 percent to 1,382 percent higher than what Medicare would pay for those same services.

Health Affairs reports almost 20 percent of inpatient hospital admissions starting in the ER lead to unexpected bills. New York's Department of Financial Services told CNBC that surprise bills from out-of-network radiologists in 2012 averaged $5,406, of which insurers paid $2,497 on average.

Consumers were on the hook for the remainder.

If you live in a rural area, call now to see if your hospital has any ER doctors on your health plan. Most of them are not, so they would be deemed out-of-network. Do the same for anesthesiologists.

Laboratory work is huge out-of-network bill waiting to happen. Ask your insurer for which labs they cover, and demand that all of your lab work goes there.

> Lab work is a huge out-of-network bill waiting to happen.

If a doctor ever says, "I'll take whatever your insurance pays," go to another doctor because this is illegal. You could get a big bill you don't expect yet be legally obliged to pay. Such debt is unfair.

Hidden Medical Debt

Medical debt is only one type of what we call "debt of necessity." This is an unexpected expense to meet unexpected emergencies and living expenses. Such debts could include payday loans for replacing worn-out tires on the car or for putting food on the table.

More than 50 percent of our fellow citizens in this great country chronically have at least two of three criteria RIP uses to determine debt forgiveness: Low earnings, zero net worth, high out-of-pocket medical expenses as a percentage of gross income.

We wonder how people get by. Well, a lot of them don't. Some 15 million people annually lose their life savings because of medical debt. When it comes to medical bills, thanks to our broken system, crowdfunding has become the insurance policy of last resort. How often can we appeal to our friends and family to rescue us?

VA-Covered Veterans

Heaven forbid that a veteran does not pay for any non-covered benefits and winds up owing the VA! The federal government has collection powers that far exceed anything banks or creditors have as enforcement tools. The "right of offset" means that, regardless of hardship or ability to pay, tax refunds may be garnished to pay off any federal and state liabilities still due.

As for bills veterans owe to the Veterans Health Administration, the government can and will offset not only a tax refund but also monthly benefits. They can offset a medical bill, for example, even if that leaves a veteran with only $25 to live on for the month.

VA members account for more than two million visits a month at non-VA hospitals. Their VA insurance, just like everyone else's, covers only so much. All remaining balances are called "self-pay." If these cannot be handled, the next step is the bill collector.

RIP is concerned about more than $8 billion in medical debt that VA members owe over the last five years from ambulance and ER bills denied for payment by the VA. We learned this by visiting the House Committee on Veterans' subcommittee on health. Denied VA benefits, the claims fall to veterans to pay. If not, the ambulance service or hospital must absorb a loss or pursue collections.

About 90,000 veterans a year are denied coverage by the VA's "prudent layperson" standard. For example, the VA may rule that an ambulance trip and hospital ER visit wasn't really an emergency. An audit found many denials are due to inconsistent application of policy and standards. The denials save the VA about $3 billion each year, burying our vets in mountains of debt.

Remove Material Hardship

What if paying for medical bills was not so stressful, if it did not result in material hardship or financial ruin, so high medical costs do not destroy us and our citizens? Research shows that any person paying more than 2.5 percent of their gross income for out-of-pocket medical expenses feels hardship. At least 20 percent of us are in hardship with medical debt on our credit reports.

This means we don't have to wipe out medical debt completely. We have to remove the material hardship tied to it. Reducing hardship to maximize wellbeing is

> **Any person paying more than 2.5 percent of their gross income for out-of-pocket medical expenses feels hardship.**

what RIP seeks to do by wiping out unpayable medical debt — debt of necessity brought on by injury, illness or violence.

We are now learning how to do it better through an academic randomized control trial of the economic impact of medical debt and debt relief. *Does debt forgiveness actually improve wellbeing?* We are researching that presently. Foundations and policymakers are awaiting the findings in 2019.

People who have not suffered hardship, poor health or poverty might think medical debt is the "fault" of its disadvantaged people. The evidence points elsewhere. Medical debt can happen to anyone, any strata or race, no matter how many assets you have.

Firsthand Material Hardship

Over the first five years of RIP Medical Debt's existence, my family has experienced prolonged poverty with major out-of-pocket expenses due to illness and material hardship. Medical debt has had a major impact on my own family's finances.

Two years after Jerry Ashton and I started this charity in 2014, my spouse asked me a simple question: "Why are we going into debt and hardship to get people out of debt?"

The answers I gave my wife were not an explanation based on logic or self-preservation. I had to seek advice from friends to help resolve this in myself. My determination to keep going was against my family obligations as a provider. My pastor helped me with my dilemma. I'm grateful my family persevered in tough times.

From the stress of three years of financial uncertainty, my wife entered the hospital. We hocked all of her family jewelry and silver. (I am glad to say I could return my wife's precious family heirlooms after them being gone more than a year, thanks to RIP attracting a better cashflow after John Oliver.) We used up all of our savings. We borrowed tens of thousands from friends and family.

To withstand my not having income for almost three years, we sold our home and used the proceeds. We rented for half of what we were paying for the mortgage. We incurred "debt of necessity" equal to three times "our" income (my spouse's teaching assistant income). At least we still had health insurance. My credit report rating fell because of one missed payment — yes, missed by one day — and we could not get parent-PLUS student loans that year for our college-age children. Two of my sons put their college education on hold. One dropped out from all the stress of rising early to work in the cafeteria at 5 a.m., before classes, to pay off an exorbitant installment loan agreement.

> Two years after starting RIP, my wife asked, 'Why are we going into debt to get people out of debt?'

Can you imagine the hardship of living on your spouse's income, below the poverty level, with a family of six, for over two years, with no more savings, and you are in your mid-fifties?

By RIP's criteria, the Antico family was qualified for RIP's debt forgiveness! (RIP can't yet forgive individuals' debt.) Our income fell to below two times the poverty level. We were insolvent. We had out-of-pocket medical expenses or debt equal to more than five percent of the family gross income.

This is not a victim story. It's my own narrative of what it took for RIP to exist and start to flourish. Compared to the tales of illness, poverty and hardship we read in letters and emails arriving daily, the Antico family had it easy. (Don't tell my wife I wrote that!)

Was putting my family in jeopardy for RIP the right thing to do? No. It was what I *had* to do. Jerry made his own sacrifices as RIP lived on his credit cards. We both went into personal debt. Why? We could not in good conscience walk away from all those with medical debt that we were uniquely equipped to help.

Where else in the world could you ever hope to find two former collections industry executives willing to reverse their career course, deciding not to collect on medical debt but to forgive it?

More than two years in, by the time of the John Oliver show, we had reached a level of forgiving almost $40 million in medical debt for 30,000 individuals who otherwise could never pay off those bills. We could not and would not stop. Our personal finances stank, but we were hooked on abolishing medical debt. For good.

CHAPTER 4

The John Oliver Effect

Jerry Ashton

RIP Medical Debt is being brought to you courtesy of comedian John Oliver.

RIP first came to America's attention in June 2016 through his satirical lambast of the debt buying and collections industry, aired on the HBO series, "Last Week Tonight with John Oliver."

The experience ever since for Craig Antico, Robert Goff, and me bordered on being surreal, and this continues today.

Overnight, after two years of basic survival (the venture funded by personal debt), our little startup charity was no longer struggling. Overnight, people heard about us, got involved, and we grew.

I want to tell you that story.

Thanks to John Oliver's very public introduction, thanks to the generosity of thousands of donors since his HBO show, thanks to our hard work pulling together a passionate and dedicated team, by the end of 2018, RIP has been able to purchase and forgive almost a half billion dollars in unpayable medical debt. A quarter of a million Americans have experienced unexpected freedom from medical debt they thought would never be paid. We hope to do more.

John Oliver on LWT routinely exposes the flaws and absurdities of politicians, extremists, miscreants, and industries whose practices appear unhinged from ethics or common sense. His "Debt Buyers" segment revealed (to many for the first time) how personal debt is purchased and collected, including debts more than ten years old or out-of-statute. He ridiculed the states that do not regulate or license debt-buying companies.

To make his case, he showed an old video of a known "bad apple" in the collections trade. Oliver poked fun at the collector's brazen attitude and his shady tactics. The audience laughed, yet they also cringed.

Becoming a debt buyer himself, once inside the industry, John Oliver was aghast at his unfettered access to thousands of people's personal data for sale as medical debt.

> **John Oliver was aghast at his unfettered access to personal data for sale as medical debt.**

The show's "hook" was to "out-Oprah Oprah." In 2004, Oprah Winfrey had famously given a studio audience nearly 300 brand new cars, valued at more than $2 million. ("You get a car! You get a car!") To surpass that record, Oliver's team set up an elaborate plan to buy and give away $15 million in medical debt.

At the climax of the live show, Oliver pushed a giant red button and glittering confetti came streaming down. He lifted his arms and rejoiced, "I am the new queen of daytime talk!"

John Oliver lampooned a shadow finance industry while freeing about 9,000 people from financial hardship by RIP forgiving their medical debt. To pull it off, he employed two former bill collectors, Craig and me. That irony made the fun all the more delicious.

How did this life-changing event come about?

A Deal Was Done

To show how easy it is to buy and collect debt, LWT producers created a debt-buying company and purchased a batch of Texas debt for about $60,000. Their intent, for comedic and ethical purposes, was not to collect on the debt but to forgive it. How?

The HBO team sought help from a healthcare attorney, Michele Masucci, a partner at Nixon Peabody. She responded to questions about ways to dispose of the debt. ("No, you can't do that, or that, either.") So that the forgiven debt did not count as taxable income, she said, they needed a tax-exempt charity with the expertise to meet the HIPAA "permissible use" rules for medical accounts.

On her desk was a copy of *The Patient, The Doctor and The Bill Collector,* by Robert Goff and me. Robert is RIP's first board member. As her client, Robert had gifted her the new book a few days before. Michele turned to the chapter, "Got Medical Debt? Let's Abolish It!" She said to HBO, "These are the people you need to see."

HBO called Robert, who referred them to Craig and me. We met at HBO's Manhattan offices. All the right people sat around a table. All the right questions were asked and answered. After the flurry of due diligence, all the right things proceeded to happen.

A deal was done.

LWT would donate to RIP Medical Debt its almost $15 million debt portfolio plus sufficient funds to process the accounts and mail the forgiveness letters. The broadcast would air in two weeks.

Mum's the word.

The night of the show, June 5, 2016, my wife and I sat before the TV in our apartment. Two glasses and a split of Champagne sat on a table before us, just in case RIP's name was even mentioned. In the climactic moments, behold, RIP's logo appeared over John Oliver's right shoulder. He pointed to it, acknowledging RIP as the charity chosen to abolish the debt. We popped our cork!

Our website was not prepared for the surge of visitors generated by the show that night. It crashed! The server was overwhelmed by visitors wanting to learn more about RIP. The contact form flooded with praise for RIP, offers to donate, cries for help. Overnight, our tiny two-person venture was compelled to transform from a charity "just getting by" into a credible and recognized organization.

The John Oliver Effect Begins

Despite our readiness glitches, several thousand dollars quickly flowed in along with commitments for more. Most unexpected was the flood of interest from organizations, companies and academia desiring to partner with RIP in our work.

What we later called "The John Oliver Effect" had begun.

RIP was initially contacted by Francis Wong, a doctoral student in economics at the University of California at Berkeley. "I was really impressed by what I saw on that TV show, and my department would like to know if we could work with you to create an economic impact study of the impact of abolishing medical debt."

His offer was immediately and enthusiastically accepted.

A week later came a second call, this time from Ray Kluender, a doctoral student in economics at MIT. He made a similar request. In response, we happily introduced him to Francis.

A month later, Craig and I were invited to the North America conference of the Abdul Latif Jameel Poverty Action Lab (J-PAL), the MIT-based global research center working to "reduce poverty by ensuring that policy is informed by scientific evidence." We were asked to present an explanation of RIP's work and mission as it relates to reducing poverty.

J-PAL asked us to explain RIP's work and mission.

After our session, we were approached separately by Wes Yin, Ph.D., associate professor of public policy at UCLA, and by Neale Mahoney, Ph.D., assistant professor of economics at the University of Chicago. Francis and Ray, meet Wes and Neale!

The four academics decided to team up to conduct a study titled "The Burden of Medical Debt and the Impact of Debt Forgiveness." RIP now found itself affiliated with four outstanding academicians at four major universities, partnering with us for serious evidence-based research on the impact of medical debt forgiveness.

We felt excited, but we still had no clue of what lay ahead.

Technology Allies Appear

One/Zero Capital founder and CEO Vishal Garg felt intrigued by the John Oliver segment and reached out to us. Finding our work congruent with his corporate mission, he invited RIP to share desk space at their offices in New York City. Any office space at all was a big step up for us. We'd been working out of coffee shops and our homes, Craig in Rye and me in Manhattan.

One/Zero connected us to the TheNumber management team, who provided a data platform to use in locating and buying medical debt, plus a way to process large batches of accounts for forgiveness. Their technology, data scientists and manpower relieved us from all the manual processing that Craig and I had been doing. Suddenly, we gained the infrastructure to forgive a lot more debt!

Paul Wallis and Fergus Cloughley at OBASHI then contacted us, offering the next essential technology to be added to the RIP charity. OBASHI (Ownership, Business processes, Applications, Systems, Hardware, Infrastructure) is a method of data process modeling and mapping for enterprises, developed in Scotland by Paul and Fergus. Their solutions addressed RIP's need for data security and control.

How did they hear of us? You already know the answer.

The data integrity we'd gained with OBASHI, Craig and I saw, could transform RIP's ability to forgive medical debt, accelerating the volume of accounts we could process. Our charity could develop new ways of working with debt buyers, hospitals and associations. We could better leverage donations to abolish more debt.

Upstreaming and Health Begins

We next attracted the attention and partnership of a respected Southern California physician, Rishi Manchanda, M.D, known for his TED talk on "upstreaming." He sent us this email:

"Like many others, I imagine, I recently learned of your work through the John Oliver TV show. I am deeply interested in the intersection of health, financial security/literacy, and medical debt, especially for working families. I am active in advocacy and policy efforts to transform healthcare at local and national levels."

Dr. Manchanda encourages doctors to consider the "upstream" social and environmental conditions that contribute to sickness, and likely to medical debt. He introduced Craig and I to the idea that "social determinants" affect health.

What are *social determinants*? "Resources that enhance quality of life can have a significant influence on population health outcomes," states the U.S. Office of Disease Prevention and Health Promotion. These include such resources as safe and affordable housing, access to education, public safety, the local availability of healthy foods, local emergency and health services, and safe local environments that are "free of life-threatening toxins."

He explained to us how social factors benefit or damage health. Poverty often means an inability to afford adequate shelter, good food and quality medical care. Even if people are fortunate enough to afford healthy groceries, they may live in a "food desert" where fresh produce and unprocessed foods are simply not available.

Dr. Manchanda told us of his suspicion that owing medical debt is a social determinant of poor health; thus, he contacted us a month after spotting RIP on the John Oliver show.

The doctor was then working as Chief Medical Officer of a large, privately owned and self-insured Southern California employer. In managing two employee clinics, he was seeking innovative ways to positively affect employee health "upstream" to deter the incidence of illness. He said that in talking with his ailing employee patients, many times, too many times, the issue came up of oppressive debt. He heard woeful tales of being chased by bill collectors.

> Dr. Manchanda told us of his suspicion that owing medical debt is a social determinant of poor health.

Dr. Manchanda tested the efficacy of RIP's intervention by having his company fund a purchase of $2.1 million worth of medical debt in the geographical area where lived most of his rural patients, migrant farm workers. The campaign was not a "proof of concept," but it was a breakthrough for RIP — the first time we'd applied our "random act of kindness" to a specific locale and population, but not be the last.

Dr. Manchanda subsequently left his employer to launch Health Begins, based in Studio City. He circled back to RIP and its tools. In February 2017, Rishi used RIP to buy another $2 million in medical debt for the people of Los Angeles and Ventura counties.

He organized The Campaign to End Medical Debt, a nonprofit coalition of clinicians, advocates and academics. They raise funds to bring public attention to the importance of medical debt forgiveness as a "downstream" intervention to reduce and prevent poverty.

If we cannot easily remove people from poor areas where there is a mountain of medical debt, we realized through his campaign, at least we can begin to remove the mountain.

Pensacola Debt Sharks

At about the same time, two Florida high school students, Samir Boussarhane and Falen McClellan, wrote to say they had decided to emulate John Oliver and raise funds to abolish medical debt in their hometown of Pensacola. Could we help them? Of course!

Craig negotiated project terms with their high school to provide teacher oversight and ensure their efforts would fit the requirements of their special International Baccalaureate (IB) Program.

The Pensacola Debt Sharks, as they called themselves, sought to raise the $10,000 needed to abolish $1 million in local medical debt in the Pensacola-Mobile region. With pizza sales and after-school game nights, they earned local publicity (and a Huffington Post blog by me), which motivated an anonymous donor to make a generous contribution. All in all, the pair raised more than $30,000 to abolish $3 million in unpaid medical bills.

Their efforts earned the pair a George Washington Community Award from the Freedoms Foundation at Valley Forge.

Economic Impact Study

Six months after the HBO show, in January 2017, the university team came to New York City for a "mini-summit' we convened for them with RIP's technology, legal, and data scientist resources. We helped them formulate the practical structure needed to conduct a randomized controlled trial (RCT) for the economic study.

RIP's newest partner, TransUnion Healthcare, agreed to perform data analytics for the study. RIP and TheNumber would handle debt forgiveness tasks. J-PAL and others would fund the research.

The goal: Provide credible evidence of the economic and social impact of medical debt forgiveness.

Craig's and my years in the debt industry, and two years at RIP, had convinced us that medical debt hurts people. (This book details these impacts.) Still, does debt relief improve lives? To what extent does medical debt adversely affect people's financial wellbeing? Do people's lives really improve when their medical debts are forgiven? What are the indisputable facts? Now we could find out.

The research is both topical and urgent. In the USA, 44 million Americans show an aggregate of $75 billion in medical debt on their credit reports. If we add all the medical debt that never shows up on credit reports, we estimate $1 trillion in U.S. medical debt.

Does debt forgiveness actually matter in an individual's life? We are seeing at RIP that medical debt locks people into a "debt trap." Are they fully liberated by debt relief? A balance sheet that compares income to medical debt does not tell the whole story. This academic study will document a range of impacts from medical debt and debt forgiveness. (A list of the outcomes being measured is in the online research registry at the American Economics Association.)

> The goal: Credible evidence on the economic impacts of medical debt forgiveness.

The evidence-based study was launched in 2017 with a projected completion in 2019. An initial report was delivered at RIP's second medical debt summit in November 2018.

UC Berkeley's Francis Wong described the study methodology. The researchers record the impact from $150 million in "randomly allocated debt forgiveness" for a group of 70,000 people. Financial outcomes in three waves of forgiveness are tracked on TransUnion credit reports. A control group of an additional 70,000 people does not get forgiveness; their debts stay in collections. Phone and mail surveys, six to 12 months after each wave, track identifiable health and quality-of-life impacts for both study groups.

The study will help RIP better target its debt forgiveness efforts to the populations that most need debt relief, he said.

There may be a more crucial byproduct from the team's work. Francis Wong cited the Oregon health insurance experiment that studied the impact of the 2008 Medicaid expansion. Those findings influenced healthcare policy nationally. The medical debt forgiveness study sample is twice the size of the Oregon study, he said, so the 2019 findings on medical debt will hold significance, and may similarly influence public policy nationwide.

Let Me Count More Ways

Other surprises came our way from the John Oliver effect.

The Better Company: GetBetter.co, a San Francisco Bay Area startup, in 2018 proposed a multistate debt forgiveness campaign, still ongoing. Better will donate to RIP revenues from the app they developed to help patients and care providers having trouble getting out-of-network claims paid by insurance companies.

Intending to "out-Oliver John Oliver," Better pledged to donate $70,000 to RIP to buy $16 million in medical debt (as compared to Oliver's $60,000 spent to buy $15 million in medical bills). Their cross-country marathon campaign will conclude in New York City, where they plan to proudly relieve John Oliver of his crown.

DvM Communications: The "Last Week Tonight" exposure also landed RIP one of the best partners we could imagine in the field of media relations — Dini von Mueffling of DvM Communications.

She and her team have launched and overseen debt abolishment campaigns in communities across the nation, generating buzz and at least $100 million in aggregate debt forgiveness. They are still going strong. Their community efforts resulted in RIP Medical Debt being named one of Town & Country magazine's Top 50 Philanthropists for 2018. Enhanced credibility!

KIRO-TV: DvM facilitated our first taste of TV news investigative reporting on medical debt and debt forgiveness, starting with Seattle's Jesse Jones on KIRO-7. The station followed up his exposé of medical debt collections in the region with a $12,500 donation for us to abolish $1 million in medical debt for folks in the area. KIRO's viewers stepped up with $40,000 more in donations to dissolve an additional $5 million in local debt. Soon after, other radio and TV stations contacted us.

> **KIRO viewers stepped up with $40,000 in donations to dissolve an additional $5 million in local debt**

NBCUniversal: Media trade reporting about KIRO caught the attention of NBCUniversal, which proceeded to donate $150,000 to abolish $15 million in medical debt through its 12 local NBC-owned stations: Boston, Chicago, Dallas/Fort Worth, Hartford, Los Angeles, Miami, New York City, Puerto Rico, Philadelphia, San Diego, San Francisco, and Washington, D.C. Much like KIRO's Seattle viewers, NBC's local viewers stepped up by raising another $150,000 for RIP to forgive another $15 million in medical debt. NBC Nightly News featured RIP in a May 2018 "Inspiring America" segment. Anchor Lester Holt interviewed Craig and reported that by then RIP had forgiven medical debt for 60,000 Americans.

Oh Ye of Great Faith

An example of good creating more good came through an email in March 2018 from the Covenant Church in Carrollton, Texas.

"I represent Covenant Church, a North Texas church with many campuses. We recently saw an NBC-TV5 News story where they partnered with RIP Medical Debt to pay off medical debt in the area. We are interested in partnering with RIP in a similar manner to forgive medical debt for families in North Texas."

> 'Good News' forgiveness of $10 million in medical debt was announced from the pulpit Easter Sunday.

A few back-and-forth calls and emails followed to clarify how RIP by now can locate debt geographically and by need. Proposing a $50,000 donation, Covenant instead donated $100,000 to abolish $10 million in Dallas debt. The "Good News" forgiveness of $10 million in medical debt was announced from the pulpit by church pastor Stephen Hayes on Easter Sunday.

Pastor Hayes told NBC-5 News that the church invests $100,000 annually in mailings to attract new members for their growing and diverse congregation. "Historically, a lot of churches have done it — where you spend upwards of six figures to send out a mailer. I don't think it's a wise investment, so we decided this year for Easter to send a different kind of mail. This [RIP] letter may not go to as many people, but it will have a much greater impact."

NBC-5 taped Hayes telling the congregation, "The $100,000 you invested in Covenant has paid off a total of $10,550,610 in medical bills. These families will get to celebrate in their homes." Referring to the debt forgiven at Easter, he rejoiced, "The bill is finished. It's been paid. It's forgiven. Gone, gone, gone, done!"

Soon after, RIP began to hear from houses of worship across the country proposing local debt forgiveness campaigns. Miracles!

I'll Drink to That

A very different and more secular website inquiry arrived in late December 2016, which opened a new realm for us to explore.

"I work with Melvin Brewing Company. We're launching a new beer next year, and our team wants to have some of the proceeds go to help pay medical debts. We're looking to raise about $300,000 and drive a ton of awareness around the issue. We've realized that we have a very loud megaphone and hope to use it for good."

We had never been "adopted" as a charity before. Craig and I do enjoy a cold one now and then, in moderation, so how could we not accept an invitation by CEO and founder Jeremy Tofte and his crew to visit their headquarters near Jackson Hole, Wyoming? Melvin brewed a special batch of the pale ale and agreed to donate 2 percent of each can sold to RIP Medical Debt. Melvin's contributions by the end of 2018 have forgiven at least $30 million in medical debt within their distribution areas from California to Massachusetts.

Our partnership has evolved. Melvin sponsored a booth for RIP at the 2018 Great American Beer Festival in Denver. They attended our second medical debt summit in New York City to provide after-summit beers for the attendees. We toast their generosity!

(In case you care to forgive medical debt, it may be useful to note Melvin first tried to "do it ourselves" by setting up their own charity. As business people, they soon realized that John Oliver had the right idea: Let RIP go through all the hassle of creating a charity, going to the debt industry to buy debt, and handling data analytics to ensure only truly needy people receive those welcome yellow envelopes.)

Community Pilot Project

A foundation friend in 2018 connected us with 2-1-1 San Diego, a nonprofit operating 24 hours a day, 365 days a year. It's Southern California's most trusted resource for access to community, health, social, and disaster services — all by dialing "211." The call is free, confidential and available in more than 200 languages.

Most relevant to RIP, 2-1-1 San Diego provides access to 6,000 services, resources and programs through an online database. If 211 callers can be identified as deserving medical debt forgiveness, RIP can put to work its analytics and forgiveness services.

We're now planning a first-of-its-kind pilot project with 2-1-1 San Diego. As envisioned, RIP will use TransUnion-based analytics to enable two participating area hospitals to automatically, instantly qualify and verify former and current patients for acceptance into a charity care program or a financial assistance program.

Once the system is in place, when a person calls 2-1-1 San Diego, they will immediately be identified (by cross-referencing both debt portfolios and hospital records) to see if they need debt forgiveness. RIP will access and search millions of accounts to locate any older debt owned by debt buyers. If we locate debt, RIP will automatically apply donor funds to buy and abolish that individual's medical debt. This will be done for free.

At first, debt forgiveness will occur sporadically, and later in real time. The pilot project is a pivotal step by RIP toward being able to forgive individual medical debt on

> **This pilot project is a pivotal step toward being able to forgive individual medical debt on request.**

request. We long ago created a free Debt Forgiveness Registry at our website to prepare for a day when the capacity is in place. This pilot project may bring individual debt forgiveness closer to reality!

The Second Summits

In early November 2018, RIP convened two major summits on medical debt. On Friday we covered the status of U.S. medical debt. Saturday concentrated on military and veterans' medical debt.

A diverse collection of attendees came from across the nation to study the problem of healthcare debt and work towards solutions. They represented health insurance, collections, medical debt buyers, credit reporting agencies, health technologists, Consumer Finance Protection Bureau (CFPB), Congressional Healthcare Task Force, lobbyists, veterans, economists, and healthcare practitioners.

Both days were magical. The attendees put aside their industry labels, "positions" and agendas, so everyone could work together to resolve problems without defending turf. Our open conversation let everybody listen, speak and be heard with respect.

All returned to their organizations with agreements to support the varied teams formed to continue their summit work. On Sunday, the RIP contingent marched in the New York Veterans Day Parade. This year we had a small float. My heart filled with hope.

A Quarter Billion in Debt Relief

A married couple of substantial means saw us on John Oliver and considered making a donation. They checked us out through their C-Suite connections in Silicon Valley. Has anyone heard about this RIP Medical Debt? Are these guys legitimate?

Like an unexpected billiards bank shot, their confirming source was a Better Company investor who enthused all about how RIP was fulfilling our role in their campaign. Thanks to this reference, RIP got the thumbs-up. We engaged in a lively phone conversation with the couple and secured a small contribution, starting a relationship. And what a relationship it's been!

This fine couple, choosing anonymity, in November 2018 made a seven-figure donation to RIP that empowered us to purchase and abolish a quarter of a billion dollars ($250 million) in medical debt during the last two months of 2018. Unprecedented!

Rolled out in stages, the first $150 million of debt was eliminated in early November, including $50 million in veterans and military debt. Another $50 million in debt was forgiven at Thanksgiving, and the last $50 million was abolished during the December holidays. No one expected our yellow envelope!

The campaign was the most ambitious medical debt abolishment in U.S. history, affecting nearly 100,000 individuals and families in practically every state in the country.

The Ultimate Oliver Effect

The ultimate results of the John Oliver Effect, and what amazes us all every day, are the blessings we provide for all the people whose debts have been forgiven since the LWT episode in 2016.

All the press coverage has not gone to our heads. We never forget that forgiving medical debt is our reason for being. We accept that we are merely a vehicle through which generous donors make a real difference in the lives of thousands of random people whose debts our donors let us forgive. For all this joy from being of service, we at RIP are as thankful as the recipients of debt forgiveness.

The mission driving RIP Medical Debt since 2014 is unchanged: Locate, buy and abolish $1 billion in medical debt. Amazingly, as I write, we are halfway toward that goal. We can visualize reaching it by 2020, given the energy and passion of our partners, donors and fans. When we reach that goal, we will set a new one.

The experience for us is akin to standing in front of an old-style pinball machine, replete with flashing lights and ringing bells, trying to control a careening silver orb. We have learned a little about how to use the flippers to control the direction, to hit a few bumpers to earn extra time and as many points as possible. You might say that we are becoming pinball wizards (with a salute to The Who), but we do not presume to pretend we have true mastery.

Much like a pinball machine, the debt forgiveness game appears to have a mind of its own at times. Our little speeding ball bounces from pillar to post, lighting up whatever it encounters, including us. It certainly has lit up our future as a charity.

A deeper truth is that no matter how awed we feel by the open generosity of astounding friends, RIP Medical Debt and random debt forgiveness cannot solve all the economic and social problems of medical debt. We want to help transform healthcare itself.

Meanwhile, we do our best to draw attention to the issue of debt, hoping to stimulate the creative juices of governments, corporations and foundations to agree on solutions. This is how public policy gets formulated, we're learning. (If you happen to be one of these "major players," well, we'd love to be invited into the conversation.)

RIP continues to evolve as a charitable organization. We've now grown from three founders to a distributed team of twenty, working though our office at Serendipity Labs in New York. As we forgive our first billion in debt and start on that second billion, we will continue being profoundly grateful for the blessings of the John Oliver Effect in the lives of those struggling with unpayable medical bills.

NOTE: Craig Antico contributed to this chapter.

*What can be added to the happiness
of a man [woman] who is in health, out of debt,
and has a clear conscience?*

— Adam Smith

CHAPTER 5

Debt Is in the Details

Craig Antico

When I co-created RIP Medical Debt in 2014 with my partner and now co-author, Jerry Ashton, our purpose was and has always been to achieve a forthright, audacious goal: Raise money to buy unpaid and unpayable medical debt, and then forgive that debt to benefit the neediest debtors.

On the surface, simple enough.

In performing this service, we have learned the truth of saying, "The devil is in the details." It exactly fits our work and our mission. That simple. That hard. People tell us they love the goal of removing medical debt burdens from distressed people who need and deserve charitable debt relief. Our donors, partners and sponsors naturally want and need to understand the details, as may you.

Precisely what does RIP Medical Debt do? How do we go about locating, qualifying and forgiving medical debt? Where and how is medical debt located? Who owns someone's personal medical debt, and how does that come about? When does medical debt enter the "secondary debt" market? Why is so much medical debt still owed? Does medical debt ever go away? Is it really a hardship? Why?

To answer these questions, I first need to provide more history. We knew early that RIP needed a clear business case that resonated with donors: Forgive as much unpayable medical debt as we can.

As two former collections industry executives, we are uniquely positioned to raise public awareness about how medical debt harms millions of Americans and our nation as a whole.

People agree that medical debt is a wrong that needs correcting. They hear about us and then say, "Tell me more." They discover that healthcare costs are the leading cause of personal bankruptcies, causing 15 million people and their families to go insolvent yearly. The more people learn, the more they want to help.

This is how and why, as of publishing this book, RIP is almost halfway to our initial goal of abolishing $1 billion in healthcare debt. Is this big news? It's a drop in the bucket. Can we do more?

Well, let's get into those devilish details.

Does Medical Debt Ever End?

If you owe a relative or friend money that you promised to pay back, do you think that debt ever goes away? Fifteen years from now, any unpaid debt lingers between you, so you may isolate yourself from that person. You might feel anxious, guilty, ashamed, upset, or disappointed that you couldn't, wouldn't, didn't know how, or have been plain incapable of paying them back. From a legal standpoint, the debt is still owed, even after the statute of limitations expires. Ethically, the debt remains due. A promise is a promise.

Exchange your friend for a hospital or another medical provider. Does a bill you owe ever go away? No. You have four options:

1. You or another can pay the medical debt in-full or settle it.
2. The provider can issue a credit to cure the debt or forgive it.
3. The debt can be "discharged" by a U.S. bankruptcy court.
4.. The debt can be "extinguished" by law, a voided contract.

Those are your four options. Unless one of those events occurs, you still owe a debt until the day you die, but then only if your estate is insolvent, or if you don't live in one of nine U.S. states where debt is inherited. Generally, medical debt never goes away.

What if a hospital told you they wrote off your bill as bad debt? What if they changed their billing system and stopped sending you statements? What if a doctor agreed to take whatever your insurance company pays? What if that bill is 15 or 20 years old?

Sorry. In all likelihood, your medical bill is still owed.

Is this ethical or morally right? Realistically, can any debt be valid when those owing it, no matter how hard they work to be personally responsible, can never pay it back in their lifetime?

This is the reality with medical debt.

Whom can we blame for the egregious injustice and burden of medical debt? Do we blame the "healthcare system," the creditors, care providers, or loan originators? Do we blame the patients, blame the victims? For me, laying blame does not solve the problem.

To eliminate that onus, in my view, some unpayable debt in the health care system should be canceled, extinguished, as if it never existed in the first place. I hope for a day when medical debt does not persist in America, but getting to that point is a debate!

Until that remote day, debt is debt. Until that day, RIP will keep contacting medical debt owners to locate all the debt we can buy and abolish by forgiving it. This is our "fairness doctrine."

Companies call RIP offering to sell us their "receivables" or "assets," which is what your debts are to them. Knowing debt never dies and government constantly shifts the playing field, they call us to protect their patients, their

> In all likelihood, your medical bill is still owed.

customers (or themselves) from liability for future collections. They know that if a company goes bankrupt, a trustee has superpowers to demand payment from all debtors, no matter how old the debt.

Ever hear the term "zombie" debt? In our industry, this is a debt that bounces from agency to agency, debt buyer to debt buyer, and never seems to go away. Too often, a third-party debt collector convinces a hospital or provider to place their oldest unpaid accounts with them, promising they will only charge a collection fee for those bills if they collect. That old debt gets new life. Patients who thought their bills were dead suddenly start getting collection calls.

> 'Zombie' debt never dies or goes away.

What if you pay all or part of your medical debt with a credit card, bank loan or payday loan? What if you default upon that creditor? Once they exhaust all their collection activity and mark you as a loss, they may formally forgive the debt or settle it in part. Whew! You think the debt is no longer owed, but there's a catch.

The government considers the amount you did not have to pay as ordinary income. The creditor sends you a 1099-C "Cancellation of Debt Income" (CODI) with a copy to the IRS. You must pay taxes on that "income." For instance, the government annually forgives $110 billion in student loan debt. If you are so "lucky," watch for a 1099-C in the mail. You may owe taxes for income you never saw.

Unintended Consequences

This book could aptly be named "End Medical Debt Hardships" because medical debt never goes away, not legally, ethically, or as a burden on people's minds. Medical debt is a hardship. That is why we seek to buy and forgive as much medical debt as we can (what we call "debt of necessity"), no matter its age or legal status.

To show what we deal with at RIP, take the statute of limitations (SOL). States have an "out-of-statute" time limit on when a creditor can collect money owed through a lawsuit (or the threat of one). The SOL can range from two or three years to more than 10 years. Many think after the statutory time limit is over, collections stop, and the debt is extinguished. That is a common misperception.

Some states go further to protect the consumer. Mississippi has strengthened SOL rules, so now debts are automatically extinguished after three years. If this becomes the law elsewhere, we expect to see sharp changes in the ways hospitals charge their customers and how quickly they collect those medical bills.

If government consumer protection laws or regulations limit the time creditors can collect accounts, the inevitable "unintended consequences" might be disastrous.

If we end people's ability to pay credit (medical debt) over time, and demand payment upfront in cash, expect access to healthcare (or any service or product) to be severely impacted.

This could result in a complete "outsourcing" of care financing away from care providers to disconnect patient-doctor relationships. Outsourced medical bills then would be owed to a finance company or bank, not the provider, just as if you used a credit card. If you had pay medical bills up front, most will use credit cards, yet consumers are warned against using credit cards to pay medical bills.

Imagine what would happen if hospitals were "forced" to bring credit finance companies into their hospitals. It's possible patients would owe banks at least $800 billion a year.

Only 10 percent of medical debt is reported to credit bureaus, tallying $75 billion. That would change. Banks, by law and industry standards, would be required to report all that $800 billion to credit bureaus. This would appear on reports as "other" consumer credit, not as medical debt. Credit cards buy big-screen TVs and vacations, right? Not so! We estimate at least 20 percent of the almost $900 million owed on credit cards is for medical OOP expenses.

People with medical debt on their credit reports already have about 70 percent more credit card debt than those without medical debt. Wisconsin's experiment, just as any finance company or bank takeover of medical billing, suggests the unintended consequences from the most well-intentioned healthcare regulations.

Uncollectable Medical Bills

Hospitals that cannot collect on accounts owed by individuals who are qualified for charity care or Medicaid (but did not sign up) are vexing to both the hospital and the collection agent.

Hospitals collect unpaid bills internally if they have the means to do so, but accounts are often placed for collection to comply with regulations. These accounts likely will become "bad debt."

To keep a 501(c)(3) status, hospitals needs to meet Community Benefit Requirements. A hospital must show the U.S. government they're supporting the needy and those in hardship. My experience, however, shared by others in the medical debt industry, is that more than one-third of the accounts assigned for collections should have qualified for charity care. A hospital's "account misclassification" problem becomes an unintended consequence of the regulations intended to protect healthcare consumers!

Hospitals cannot sell to debt buyers the accounts that collection agencies declare as uncollectible. Hospitals must take the "hit." That hardly resolves the debt problem for patients. They enter purgatory. Although the hospital appears to have stopped collecting on the old debt, the patients still know they owe the amount.

Such debt makes up the lion's share of all the medical bills owed by consumers that are now in third-party collections. This is where we come in at RIP as debt buyers and forgivers.

How Is Debt Bought?

To understand how we can abolish debt for good, you first need to understand how it's bought by investors to make money.

Medical billing accounts you owe, like mortgages, can be bought and sold. At a profit, of course. Collection executives recover money for a living. The debt-buying executives who invest in debt portfolios need to buy debt at a price where they can profit, expecting to collect two to three times the amount they pay. If they buy a portfolio of debt for $10,000, they expect to collect $20,000 to $30,000.

All hospitals and most physicians use collection agencies to help collect money owed by their patients after the insurance company has paid its portion. Hospitals staff their collection departments so each collector has 8,000 accounts to handle at any one point in time. Staff overwhelm leads to unpaid accounts being placed with third-party collection agencies. The Association of Credit and Collection Professionals International says there are 100,000 bill collectors in the USA, and more than half of them collect medical debt.

Suppose that some debt buyer uses the same collection agency as a hospital. The question becomes, "Why wait for a collection agency to collect before we get our part?" A business needs cash to operate. "Accounts receivable" are not cash unless or until collected.

Half of all bill collectors now collect medical debt.

Debt buyers bring needed capital to debt sellers, so these creditors need not wait two, three or four years to finally get their money, if ever. Debt buyers are sophisticated, with strong dispute resolution skills and respectful collection practices. There is no room in their world for unethical practices, not like what we hear about. The debt industry has shifted toward treating debtors with respect.

Debt bought from hospitals is seldom bought for pennies on the dollar, as RIP pays. Prices are closer to five, 10, 15 cents or more on the dollar, depending on the billing accounts' age, the likelihood of successfully contacting patients and the likelihood of collecting from them. As a business, debt buyers take on such risk, aware they might not collect two to three times the amount they paid.

If a debt buyer pays $50 for each $1,000 bill owed, for example, they have to collect $150 to $200 per $1,000, on average, to make an acceptable return for the risk assumed by them, their bankers and investors. They may collect on "fresh" accounts fairly quickly, yet it can take three to 10 years to collect from the remaining accounts — three to 10 years of phone calls, letters, and even lawsuits.

More than seven percent of all workers in the USA have income garnishments. Most are for child support or alimony, yet more than 25 percent of those garnishments are from medical debt judgments, often in cases filed by debt buyers.

We at RIP can cost-effectively buy portfolios of accounts from medical providers and debt buyers because we research the accounts deeper than they do. We are debt buyers who are not economically constrained by profit. We care only about the social profit.

Which Debt Is Bought?

Our strategic partner, TransUnion Healthcare, believes in what we are doing — using their information for good. We use their data, plus publicly available data, plus purchased social determinant data, for identifying the portfolios to buy. We try to get the best possible picture of patients in the context of their debts and situations. With this data, we can better value a portfolio, measure the impact of debt forgiveness. We do this not to ensure that our donors don't overpay, but to ensure that the people who most need help get our debt relief. We become, essentially, debtors' second-chance safety net.

Once we identify debtors needing our help, such as where a local group does a community debt forgiveness campaign, our next step is buying their debt. At this point, we may seek a medical provider willing to sell us their unpaid debt at a charitable price. More likely, we go into the *secondary medical debt market*. There we locate debt and run it through our data analytics, so we are confident of buying only accounts that qualify for our charity work. We then negotiate a price for a portfolio and take possession by paying for it.

As the legal owners of a debt, we can legitimately extinguish it.

What we do with debt differs from what collection agencies do. Penniless accounts, for collectors, are nuisances they place on credit reports on the chance one day a debtor will get a job or inheritance, so monies appear to pay it, plus interest and charges, just to clear the debt from credit reports and be done with it.

We buy account portfolios from debt sellers at a steep discount off the amount originally owed to a medical provider. From the date of debt purchase, *our work is the reverse of a collection agency.* We abolish the debt in full, no strings attached. We make sure the credit blemish is removed — all within 90 days of buying that debt.

> **RIP buys debt at a steep discount off the amount owed to a medical provider.**

Such debt purchases can only be done in volume. If RIP tried to buy one account at a time, we'd have to pay 50 times the $5 to $15 for each $1,000 account we pay now. That's too much for us. This why our charity cannot forgive debt for any individuals on request. Not yet. Maybe someday. We created a Debt Forgiveness Registry for that future day we figure out how.

Our success comes only in partnership with donors and debt sellers (maybe you). Medical debt forgiveness occurs when we join with those who want to free fellow humans from undue destructive circumstances. No judgment, no pity. Just a gift from one stranger to another. Our role is to facilitate that affirmation of care.

Also required is a hospital, doctor or debt owner willing to sell or donate accounts to us rather than continuing to collect internally or park bills at a collection agency. Imagine the pleasure of a hospital or provider after donating, or selling for pennies, something of little value in return for changing a patient's life for the better.

We and our donors —"social investors"— agree: A collection process that takes three to 10 years to complete is too long and too socially destructive. We aim to remove hardship from debtors by taking the investor and the bill collector out of the picture, generally after the second or third year of a bill. We work through the market pricing system, not through legislation. Our business careers help us to pay below-market rates to take medical debt off the street.

Community Benefit Requirements

Charity care is only one required community benefit a hospital offers its patients in return for state and federal tax exemptions. On average, hospitals spend about six percent of their revenues upon improving the health of their community.

A tax-exempt charitable hospital can receive significant benefits if they comply with IRS and state regulations. Part of meeting their role in providing community benefits is demonstrating initiatives, activities, and investments they've undertaken to improve health in the community. Hospitals can also lose their federal tax exemption if they do not comply with the rules.

Within these requirements awaits an opportunity. As distilled from Plante Moran, here is an overview:

- The hospital must conduct a local "Community Health Needs Assessment" (CHNA). and adopt an "implementation plan" that addresses the needs. This must be submitted every three years. The strategic plan must be adopted on or before the 15th day of the fifth month after the year a CHNA is conducted. A $50,000 excise fine curbs non-compliance.

- The hospital must create a Financial Assistance Policy (FAP), publicized in the community, and an emergency medical care policy on providing care without regard to FAP eligibility.

- The hospital must limit amounts charged under the FAP to no more than the amounts billed to individuals who have insurance.

- The hospital is prohibited from collection actions against an individual without reasonable efforts to determine FAP eligibility.

> Hospitals can lose their federal tax exemption if they don't comply with benefit rules.

Tax-exempt hospitals report four items on their Schedule H to document how they benefit their communities:

1. Financial assistance and means-tested government programs.
2. Community building activities.
3. Medicare shortfall fiscal report.
4. Bad debt attributable to charity care.

Meeting community benefit requirements in 2011 was worth $24.6 billion, noted Julia James at Project HOPE. That tax exemption (state and federal) was shared by 60 percent of 5,500 U.S. hospitals.

What if hospitals could count bad debt for eligible charity care as meeting their Community Benefit Requirements? As calculated from hospitals' Form 990s in 2013, this could exceed $67 billion.

With more than $30 to $40 billion at stake in the tax exemption, is health care leadership ready to act? Here is an opportunity!

A culture of care and charity starts from the top. The CEO, CFO, CMO (medical officer) and governing boards can make change happen. Is the business of health care distracting them from their main mission of helping people? Should regulations prevent hospitals from abolishing indigents' bad debt?

RIP provides an effective and sane way for hospitals to rid their books of medical debt, a "safe harbor" to end intractable problems from medical debt. The potential is evident on the Schedule 990 H publicly filed by tax-exempt hospitals — at least $25 billion!

Everyone know the bad debt is still owed. Letting debt "sit on the books" doesn't make it go away, nor does it grant healthy peace of mind to those owing medical debt they cannot pay.

Community hospitals are not equipped with the cost accounting systems, analytics and reporting to provide reliable evidence that they do provide care for the needy. We are certain hospitals provide this community benefit, but they have a hard time coming up with systems-generated evidence to prove it.

Working in partnership with RIP's analytics and leveraging our tax-exempt charity status, hospitals can provide their communities with the miracle of medical debt forgiveness. The only "debt details" left to manage will be how to identify those accounts and ask RIP to put yellow debt forgiveness letters in the mail.

The cure for medical debt is in the details. For goodness' sake.

CHAPTER 6

Margin Over Mission: Head vs. Heart

Robert Goff

The healthcare industry is a huge part of the American economy. Along with spending on services, the healthcare industry is the largest source of employment in the nation.

All the trillions spent on healthcare are spread across numerous enterprises, yet it's concentrated in two components — physicians and hospitals. The American Medical Association reports these two represent just under half of all healthcare spending.

Physicians and hospitals are the most familiar to us. Hospitals are those large, imposing buildings that have been there forever, fixtures in our communities. Physicians are honored for knowledge and compassion, each a reincarnation of Marcus Welby, M.D.

While we think of them as linked, hospitals and physicians are different and separate economic units. How each is compensated has determined how they've evolved, and how they evolved greatly impacts healthcare costs. All of these costs outstripping the ability of patients to pay is what creates medical debt.

The Urge to Merge

Consolidating economic power is increasing healthcare costs.

The structure of healthcare delivery is a vestige of 19th and 20th century concepts and limits. If care required more than a physician, the hospital played a critical role as a hub of sophisticated services and technology, such as surgical services, radiology and laboratory. Before immunizations, hospitals also protected communities from communicable diseases.

Hospitals continued this local role while the world around them changed. Isolated communities were linked by roads and bridges. Populations shifted. Advances in medical science and technologies reduced the need for hospitals' core service — inpatient beds.

Hospitals survived by adapting. Between 1975 and 2015, about 1,500 hospitals closed their doors. Eliminating beds and hospitals did not slow spending. Statista reported hospital expenditures rose from $27.2 billion in 1980 to about $1.2 trillion by 2018. Said one administrator, "There is no mission without a margin."

The hospital evolved from a community charity with a mission of service into a business enterprise. To meet the public benefit mission, hospitals were licensed to guarantee competence. Licenses let hospitals become monopolies or oligarchies in their service areas. Hospitals used business techniques to control how the healthcare dollar was spent. Their license let local hospitals dominate inpatient services and then control outpatient and physician services. Hospitals became profit centers.

Hospitals next merged with other hospitals and other sectors of care delivery, like urgent care and ambulatory surgery. A "system" was created that not only dominates delivery of care but exploits it economically. Hospitals grew at the expense of communities that the hospitals' founders had pledged to serve as a mission.

Hospitals are compensated for services provided. The more the services, the greater the revenue. Hospitals are paid formula-based rates for Medicare and Medicaid. Hospitals are paid more for both Medicare and Medicaid services than independent providers.

Commercial insurance plans negotiate hospital service payments. A monopoly or oligarchy hospital system negotiates from a position of strength in the local geography. Pay the demanded rates, or don't do business with that local healthcare system.

Press releases for nearly every merger promise cost savings. After a merger, Forbes reported, prices rise upward to 44 percent.

Not every hospital dominates the local market. Hospitals with favorable Medicare rates (Medicaid rates are rarely profitable), plus a solid volume of commercially insured patients, can expand their profit margins by negotiating increased payments from insurance companies. Higher insurance payments get passed on to patients, of course, as higher insurance premiums.

Downstream Revenues

Hospital systems dominating health care delivery often feed their business interests by capturing downstream revenues. They seek to capture every healthcare dollar spent in their service area. Disney World may seek to capture every vacation dollar spent in Orlando, but hospitals do not run a risk of people vacationing elsewhere.

Profit margins are good in business. Health insurance companies in 2017 ran margins between 4.0 and 5.25 percent, says Investopedia. The American Hospital Association's TrendWatch reports hospitals enjoying 6.4 percent operating margin yet suffering negative profit margins of -23 percent. Seven of the ten most profitable hospitals in 2013 were not-for-profit institutions. Gundersen Lutheran Medical Center in La Crosse, Wisconsin, had $302 million in profits.

Hospital systems use profit margins from their "medical mission to serve" to grow bigger and dominate even more.

Health insurance companies, by law, must spend a percentage of premium revenues on healthcare services or refund policyholders. Hospitals have no such obligation to use profits for reducing their charges or for community betterment, so few do.

Profits go toward acquiring more and more medical providers, like physician practices and urgent care facilities. Hospital mergers and acquisitions tallied 115 transactions in 2017, reported RevCycle Intelligence, and the tally increased 11 percent in 2018.

Venture Capitalism

Hospitals also are entering the venture capital business. Indeed, hospitals are a new source of financing for new ideas and businesses. Forbes reported that in the first half of 2017, more than $6 billion of hospital money financed startup business ventures. Hospital systems investing in new businesses risk mission-driven revenues for future potential economic gains. The adventure can be perilous for a hospital's economic stability.

One area of investment is going head-to-head with the insurance companies. Hospital systems know healthcare best, after all, so they figure, "Why not cut out the middleman and create our own health plans? Why not capture insurance margins as our own?"

The reality is different than expected. A 2017 Allan Baumgarten study, funded by the Robert Wood Johnson Foundation, found that only four of 42 hospital health plans were profitable in 2015. Some reported significant losses, and five went out of business.

Becker's Hospital CFO Report noted that Northwell, based in Long Island, absorbed significant losses from their health insurance startup, CareConnect. Losses on a second insurance plan Northwell owned pushed the entire health system into the red by $36.2 million during the first quarter of 2017. This does not include the loss of all investment capital to launch CareConnect.

Should hospitals increase their charges and their costs to invest in risky ventures?

Premier Health in Ohio, said Dayton Daily News, shuttered its insurance plans after a three-year effort with losses of $40 million. Unable able to find a buyer, their return on investment was zero.

Some hospital systems are still pushing ahead with their health insurance ventures, plowing in hospital revenues to fund deficits. Other systems are pulling the plug, divesting themselves of losers, as did Catholic Health Initiatives in Englewood, Colorado, and Tenet Healthcare in Dallas. Such economic losses reduce the resources for the organizations providing direct health care.

I will not say if these investment strategies are good or bad. The question I raise is: Should hospital systems be able to increase their charges to private and government payers, and increase costs to the patients, to invest their resources in risky business ventures?

Private business hopes for a high return on investment (ROI), no guarantees. If a venture fails, the hit is taken by the investors, the shareholders. However, a not-for-profit hospital system has no such shareholders. Investment losses, if big enough, endanger a hospital's critical medical services. Must a community bail out a local hospital because of its appetite for investing in new ventures?

Should higher health costs, higher premiums, plus higher taxes for Medicare and Medicaid. fund a protected monopoly's attempts to expand domination over where our medical dollar is spent?

Regardless of how hospital systems use their fiscal resources, the public is expected to pick up any added care costs. Hospital systems increasingly invest revenues in self-aggrandizement — advertising. Becker's Hospital Review reported that U.S. hospitals spent an estimated $4.9 billion for local advertising in 2017.

HealthLeaders Magazine has defended marketing expenditures, saying, "Hospitals need to advertise to maintain or enhance revenue flow. Even nonprofit hospitals need to market to insured patients and promote high-grossing service lines, so that they are able to continue to care for the uninsured."

Same rationale: There is no mission without a margin.

Employed Physicians

Hospital systems grow by adding physicians as employees. How? About 80 percent of U.S. healthcare spending results from decisions made by physicians. Influence or control that care decision, and you control a significant amount of revenue. Employee physicians yield a regular flow of patients referred to ancillary services owned by the system. System-owned services are paid more than independently owned services, so boosting patient volume assures the system's overall costs for health care will rise.

Laboratory Economics reported that a UnitedHealthcare in-network hospital lab in New York charged 23 times more than did local LabCorp for the same tests ($384 versus $16.25).

Medical Economics has reported that Medicare paid $188 to an independent physician for a level II EKG without contrast. The same EKG in a hospital's outpatient setting cost 140 percent more ($452,89) when charged by the employed physician.

Costs from hospital-employed physicians are a fiscal drain on Medicare. Modern Healthcare Magazine in November 2017 ran an analysis of U.S. costs for four procedures at hospital outpatient services and independent locations. Employed physicians generated 27 percent more Medicare costs ($3.1 billion) than did the independent physicians. Employed physicians were seven times more likely to provide services in a more costly hospital outpatient setting.

> **Influence or control the health care decision, and you control a significant amount of revenue.**

An Empire BlueCross executive said the cost of care provided by an employed physician is 20 to 40 percent higher than the cost of that same care by a physician in independent practice.

Hospitals' employment of physicians is increasing dramatically. Between July 2015 and July 2016, hospitals acquired 5,000 physician practices, reported Healthcare Dive. Separately, FierceHealthcare reported that hospital-owned practices increased 100 percent in the four years ending in 2016. Nationally, 38 percent of all physician practices are now hospital-owned.

Independent Physicians

Local independent physicians are fighting a rearguard action.

Independent physician practices may be a vanishing breed, but individual physicians in small practices remain the providers of choice for most of the frequent medical care people receive.

Independent physicians face a greater economic burden than those employed by hospital-owned practices, and they have far less flexibility in revenue generation. Regulations don't favor them in atttempting financial creativity and "revenue maximization."

A 2012 American Medical Association survey of physicians shows that despite the shift to hospital employment, 53.2 percent of physicians were self-employed, and 60 percent of these in practices wholly owned by physicians. Most independent practices are in the medical specialties directly affecting the lives and wellbeing of their patients, such as family practitioners, obstetricians/gynecologists, internists, and internal medicine subspecialties like oncology.

Beyond their responsibilities for the delivery of medical care, the independent physicians must also endure the pressures and concerns of any small business owner. This includes the staff payroll. A Kaiser Foundation report, "Professional Active Physicians," estimates that small practices employ more than five million people. Each physician pays for a median of six employees. Other business costs include rent, supplies, telephone, and computers with specialized apps for all patient records and billing, plus one expense other small business owners do not have in their budgets — malpractice insurance.

> **Independent physicians must endure the pressures and concerns of any small business.**

Their source of revenue is the sale and delivery of professional expertise and specialized knowledge, generally sold in units of time. Time is a finite resource. The physicians who spend extra time with their grateful patients, in reality, put their practices at risk.

An online video, "The Vanishing Oath," narrated by Ryan Flesher, M.D, gives us a clear sense of the financial realities of the "average" physician. The average compensation for independent physicians in the USA is $146,000, three times the national average for household income. However, when you factor in overhead and working hours, physicians' take-home pay averages less than $28 an hour. It's above a minimum wage of $15 an hour, but not by much.

The average charge from more than 200 million visits paid by Medicare in 2012 was just $57, less than a plumber charges to fix a broken toilet, says Nancy Nielsen, M.D, Ph.D., a past president of the American Medical Association, as reported by MedPage Today.

Another factor in a physician's life is the burden of debt from a medical education, Student Debt Relief estimates medical students graduating in 2018 had $190,000 in debt. This affects where they choose to practice, whether they are independent or employed.

In communities where a population is economically challenged, private practice physicians are in short supply. Practice costs cannot be met through a high volume of low-paying Medicaid patients, not without the quality of care suffering. Therefore, physicians tend to congregate in high-income suburbs or upscale urban neighborhoods. Where and how physicians practice medicine becomes more about lifestyle and economics than meeting a community's needs.

Healthcare Values vs. Costs

Probably the greatest challenge facing physicians is the value that Americans place on healthcare compared with its costs. In general, healthcare costs are perceived as too high and the quality as too low. Patient satisfaction and customer service levels? Even lower.

Physicians are easy targets for efforts to control costs. They're on the receiving end of bureaucratic rules alleged to improve quality. Employed physicians have hospital resources to lessen bureaucratic burdens. Independent physicians are on their own.

Unlike other small businesses, physicians' income is largely out of their control. Businesses adapt prices to cost and competition.

> Patients are learning to match their care to their coverage.

The physicians' reimbursements are now dictated to them. Medicare pays fixed rates to physicians for seniors, the largest consumers of health care services. Each state sets its Medicaid rates. Physicians agree to accept the fixed rates from private health plans in exchange for plan participation.

Physicians in a hospital practice benefit from their monopolistic hospital assuring that its physicians are paid higher rates, but independent physicians have little leverage when negotiating with commercial health plans. For private practices, plan participation is a take-it-or-leave-it proposition.

Unique in medicine is that physicians' compensation is tied to a service or procedure, regardless of the physicians' experience, which improves the quality and efficiency of the care delivered. A surgeon removing an appendix is paid the same regardless of whether she or he is a veteran of thousands of appendectomies or a recent graduate with the ink still wet on the license. While patients want the most experienced physician, is the physician's experience being valued or respected by insurance and government plans?

Despite the perennial cry, "The sky is falling!" physicians are not dropping out of Medicare in droves. The Centers for Medicare and Medicaid Service (CMS) say that 90 percent of practicing physicians accept Medicare patients. Kaiser Health News says that 69 percent participate with Medicaid. These numbers are holding steady.

Physician participation in the commercial insurance plans is increasing while benefit coverage is shrinking or being eliminated for health services provided by physicians who do not participate with commercial plans. Patients are learning to match their care to their coverage to avoid higher out-of-pocket costs and to avoid a lack of coverage for care provided by out-of-network physicians.

Insurance companies have been less than generous in sharing their increasing premium revenue over the last ten to twelve years. MD Magazine reports on the discouraging slide of payment rates to physicians since 2001, saying they have declined or remained flat almost every year, a trend likely to continue.

Payments to physicians from commercial plans are now running less than Medicare. Between 2006 and 2013, payments dropped by about 43 percent. Medscape calculated that payment for the most common office visit is 39.8 percent less than what Medicare pays.

Patients need to understand that their physicians, all physicians, sell their time. Time remains a limited resource.

For independent physicians in private practice, their constrained reimbursements are falling behind their costs to stay in business. From 2002 to 2012, Medicare fee-for-service (FFS) rates increased 9 percent, while the cost of operating a practice — as measured by the Medicare Economic Index (MEI) — increased 27 percent, reported the Medicare Payment Advisory Commission (MedPac). The MEI includes everything from physician and staff compensation to rent, exam room tables, postage, and computers. During that very same period, the overall inflation rate was 33 percent — a net loss.

Physician-Patient Relationship

The physician–patient relationship is a unique business model. A physician is expected to provide specialized knowledge with a high degree of compassion, which is what the vast majority of physicians do, yet it poses a challenge for business viability.

A compassionate connection with patients induces independent physicians to write off unpaid bill balances, putting their practices at risk. Employed physicians' compassion for patients is the same, but they largely have removed themselves from business operations; their institutions pay other people to maximize revenue. Employed physicians traded independence for a more secure income.

Independent physicians must sustain their practice as a business, compensating their staff well enough to retain them, yet still derive a decent income themselves, so they can be there for their patients. This difficult, sometimes impossible challenge is why the number of independent physicians is diminishing.

Independent physician participate in insurance plans to support their patients. Their participation lets patients obtain the maximum coverage possible with fewer dollars coming from patients' pockets. Participation builds the physician-patient relationship by limiting fiscal pressures on that relationship. Plan participation means less income for physician, subtly straining relations with patients.

Lawrence Casalino, M.D, Ph.D., Weill Cornell Medical College, studied physician's practices and found their total cost for dealing with insurance plans was $31 billion annually — 6.9 percent of all U.S. expenditures for physician and clinical services. For patients with limited insurance coverage, or no plan coverage, considerably more time gets spent on patient-physician financial arrangements.

> Time spent on insurance could be spent on building the physician-patient relationship.

The Commonwealth Fund found physicians devoted three hours a week, three weeks a year, interacting with insurance plans. Nursing staff spent 23 weeks per year per physician. Clerical staff spent 44 weeks. This time could be spent on building the physician-patient relationship.

With care reimbursements fixed, payment sources reduced and expenses increasing, "cost-shifting" has been largely eliminated for independent physicians. Employed physicians' costs get subsidized by hospitals through referring patients to costlier ancillary services. For the independent physician, there are fewer options, and no one to help with the expense of that patient relationship.

For those with health insurance, the patient–physician financial relationship is undergoing a major change. Low copays and limited deductibles (if any) are disappearing. TransUnion Healthcare has reported that patients' average out-of-pocket costs increased 11 percent in 2017, rising to $1,813. About 39 percent of patient visits to physicians incur out-of-pocket costs from $500 to $1,000.

Origin, a healthcare analytics company, reported that the patient financial responsibility for insured individuals increased 47 percent since 2009. About 40 percent of care revenue is at risk due to patient bad-debt. This harms the physician-patient relationship.

Obamacare Impacts

The Affordable Care Act, Obamacare, increased health insurance coverage while increasing its economic burden. Obamacare added to the intensity of the patient–physician financial exchange.

The debate over "health reform" turned into a plan for getting all Americans covered by health insurance. We talked a lot about the cost of coverage but little about what it cost to obtain that coverage. Coverage did not cover everything from the first dollar onward. To get the broad coverage of the mandated benefit plans, patients had to accept higher deductibles. In theory, this would "engage" patients in realizing that care is not free, so they are judicious in its use.

In reality, cancer patients would be happy never to need services, but they have no choice. High deductibles sting the necessary users of medical care as well as the unnecessary users.

There was much talk about premium costs, how there would be tax credits for businesses to offer coverage. There would subsidies to provide for individuals to purchase coverage, and the "essential benefits" that had to be included. What it all would cost patients to access care received short shrift in the conversations.

With subsidies cushioning the economics of purchasing coverage, with essential benefits like "free" preventive care, the sticker shock of deductibles only hits us when there is an illness or injury. That's when the out-of-pocket costs can decide whether people actually choose to keep themselves or their family members healthy.

The Physician's Dilemma

High deductibles and copays become "account receivables," bad debt for physicians and medical debt for patients. Affordability is not academic for physicians in their practice. For them, it's a real challenge to their fiscal survival as well as to their ability to provide proper care for their patients.

Given the fixed or declining care reimbursements from insurance, given increased operating costs, our independent physicians face a conflict between the doctor-patient relationship and the patient-doctor financial exchange.

Physician-patient relationships give physicians more knowledge of patients' situations than the usual business transaction. This intimate knowledge of individuals' personal circumstances creates tension.

> **Physicians face a conflict between doctor-patient relationship and the patient-doctor financial exchange.**

The patients who need the most physician or other medical care and services often have the most economic issues, perhaps caused by illness or injury, or as a consequence of the stress. These patients frequently cannot work, or they're restricted in their ability to work, requiring time and attention by family members, who may decide care giving takes priority over producing income.

The physician's dilemma: With limited time to care for patients and yet produce revenue, with fixed reimbursements that limit their income, how can they balance the economic needs of their practice with a compassionate response to each patient's situation?

Head vs. Heart

Physicians in private practice must generate sufficient income to cover expenses of their practice and still support their family. When payments from insurance are insufficient, due to poor coverage or limitations on coverage, the patient is fully responsible.

Physicians know in their heads that any heart-guided write-offs of patients' debt can spell financial ruin for the practice. This struggle between the head and heart is rarely faced in other businesses.

"Hard core" bill collections against patients, who likely have both medical and financial problems, are contrary to most physicians' personal values and sentiments. Physicians will add to patients' debt load, not out of desire, but out of economic necessity.

With their heart, physicians feel an urge to forgive the debt. With their head, they know that they cannot absorb rising loses at a time of increasing expenses, nor can they risk administrative sanctions (or worse) from the insurance carriers.

What should independent physicians do? What would you do?

The easiest course is removing oneself from the business of medicine to be an employee of a large organization or institution. Free yourself to practice medicine, unburdened from the challenges of business administration, billing and collections. Turn over those distasteful tasks to your institution's financial experts. However, doing so means your patients will not be treated with your level of compassion, as billing for the services you provide go into a system designed to maximize revenue.

Billing and collections on behalf of hospital-employed physicians tend to follow the processes and programs of that institution. While every hospital has a policy for charity care, there is little outreach to ensure wise use of the funds. In fact, since the advent of the ACA, with more people being covered under Medicaid, the use of charity funds by hospitals has gone down, according to an analysis by the Advisory Board, to less than 2 percent of their operating costs.

Under Obamacare, as plan deductibles rise, the middle class suffers a gigantic increase in medical debt. This economic demographic, which mostly has insurance, just does not think of seeking charity care from local hospitals, especially at the time of service. Only when the bills arrive do the gaps in their plan coverage become evident. Only then are the tangible burdens of medical debt understood.

> **Independent physicians who choose mission over margin, put heart over head, do so at their fiscal peril.**

By then, a patient is out of the hospital. That sign in Admissions, welcoming inquiries for charity care, is not remembered. Hospitals do not go out of their way to promote charity care. A bill or demand for payment seldom offers relief by contacting the hospital.

Independent practices that sell their medical debt are few and far between, and fewer ask an agency to pursue collections in court or report bad debt to credit bureaus. However, hospital-owned medical practices, following a hospital's practices, regularly file legal action and regularly report bad accounts to credit bureaus.

Another twist causing medical debt is that the hospitals which do provide charity care, if barely, could seek better compensation rates, or community support to fund charity care. However, not-for-profit hospitals instead focus upon raising money to provide new services that increase revenue, which then increases medical debt.

Independent physicians lack institutional or community support for a heartfelt approach of absorbing the medical debt of hardship patients. There is no support for any increase in their rates, so they cannot afford to provide charity care, but many do.

Absorbing the medical debt of patients who need care but can't afford it, bluntly, is another reason to abandon private independent medical practice to join a hospital-owned practice. That choice for personal survival by independent physicians results in higher costs for health care, increasing medical debt in a community.

Independent physicians seek to provide for their patients, their employees, their own families, and their communities. They choose mission over margin, choose heart over head, yet they do so at their fiscal peril, and they alone are expected to pick up the tab.

Hospital systems tend to choose profit margin over missions of service, put mission in service of margin. Despite all the compassion of hospital leaders, institutional needs compel them to choose head over heart, to exploit every opportunity for market dominance. Our society is expected to pick up the tab. Is this sensible?

*Money is better than poverty,
if only for financial reasons.*

— Woody Allen

CHAPTER 7

Fanciful Healthcare Financing

Robert Goff

Speaking only for myself, I believe insurance is the wrong way to finance the healthcare needs of Americans.

I come to this belief honestly, only after decades in management for medical billing and collections. I do not expect you to share my opinion, yet I want to offer insightful facts, ones persuasive for me, so you can reach your own conclusions.

To understand why I say insurance is the wrong way to finance the healthcare needs of Americans, I offer here a brief education on how insurance actually works, in practical terms, and a brief history of health insurance, tracing back to war and tax policies.

Insurance is a financial device to absorb economic consequences of rare events. Insurance provides money to the policyholder to restore physical damage from a covered incident. Property insurance works well for homes and autos, so I'll use it as an example.

The financing of insurance is relatively simple. A company offers to provide coverage for these rare events. The risk is spread over all the policyholders, allowing each to pay a small amount on a regular basis toward a fund to pay any policyholder should that rare event occur. Policyholders, essentially, fund one another's losses, and the insurance company holds funds not paid out. Insurance companies, in general, prefer to be paid than to pay.

To avoid those rare events that must be covered, or to mitigate the impact, insurance companies promote safety. Policyholders are encouraged to conduct themselves in ways that reduce risk.

Insurance companies offer policyholders financial incentives to reduce claims, such as discounts for vehicle features that reduce the risk of theft or accidents. Likewise, they offer discounts for home security features, such as smoke and burglar alarms.

Policyholders assume part of the financial impact from a rare event through *deductibles*. Homeowners or car owners who become "high utilizers" of insurance coverage, or potentially high utilizers — like living in a flood plain or having a poor driving record — may find obtaining insurance coverage unaffordable or unavailable.

Lastly, homeowners' insurance policies and auto policies contain "caps" or limits on their coverage. Because homes and automobiles have market values, which can be established, insurance companies do not want to overpay for coverage. Therefore, limiting the liability of the insurance carrier is accepted in the law.

Health Care Insurance Business Model

Applying property insurance concepts to financing health care, in my view, is simply wrongheaded. An individual's need for health care is not a rare event. The need for health care is expected, perhaps predictable. Illness and injury are commonplace. Few mothers give birth today without intervention from medical services.

Health care is lifelong. A childhood rite of passage are preventive services like immunizations and checkups. In adolescence, HPV vaccinations for both genders are advised to protect against cervical and throat cancers. For young women, upon reaching maturity, a Pap test for cervical cancer is an annual ritual, as are mammograms for older women. As men mature, PSA prostate cancer screening is routine. Colonoscopies at age 50 are advised for everyone. A routine annual physical is an opportunity to screen for common measures of less-than-optional health, such as diabetes or high blood pressure. Good health insurance covers such usual and expected events in life.

The business model of covering rare events, as expected for other

> Covering rare events, the business model for other forms of insurance, does not fit for lifetime health insurance.

forms of insurance, does not fit health insurance. Unlike with a car or house, we cannot put a market value on human life.

As you age, your statistical chances increase of developing one or more chronic conditions, As medical science improves, your chances rise for living through an acute illness like appendicitis or pneumonia. Cancer treatments have now made that killer survivable for many. Cardiac surgery is considered safe and routine. Americans now live through episodic health crises that in past generations would have ended life. As we live longer, we live long enough to develop and live with chronic illnesses. We expect health insurance to cover it all.

Yes, unfortunate catastrophic and rare illnesses do occur, but 45 percent of the population, or 33 million Americans, have at least one chronic disease, reported the Partnership to Fight Chronic Disease. The Clearing House Advisory Committee calculated that chronic diseases account for the vast majority of health spending, totaling

$2 trillion in 2005. Total health care spending in 2016 surpassed $3.4 trillion. Close to 99 percent of Medicare and 83 percent of the Medicaid expenditures are necessary for chronic care.

The healthcare financing model is designed to provide financial assistance for rare events, but the system instead is expected to fund health care needs that are no longer rare, to fund needs that are not only predictable but expected. Such financing is fanciful.

High Health Insurance Premiums

The rising cost of health insurance premiums gets bashed in the healthcare debate. Critics vilify insurance company profits, big CEO salaries and wasteful administration. Often forgotten is the fact that premiums largely reflect the hard costs of medical services, the unit cost of each service, and the volume of services utilized.

Now add the cost to operate an insurance company, including claims payments, marketing, and efforts to influence utilization of services, plus a margin for profitability.

Health insurance premiums follow a simple equation:

Medical costs + administrative costs + profits = premiums.

America's Health Insurance Plans (AHIP) in 2011 reported basic industry profitability at 4.4 percent, far below the public perception that profits are in the range of 10 to 25 percent. (The average profit margin for an S&P 500 company in 2017 was 11 percent.)

To hold down their policy premiums, health insurance companies mimic the devices of property and casualty insurance to limit or mitigate their risk of claims. They encourage people to adopt healthy habits. They want us to be well.

Prior to the Affordable Care Act (Obamacare), health insurance companies often reduced their risks of medical claims by excluding coverage for preexisting conditions. They imposed waiting periods before coverage began. They excluded individuals and small groups,

> Medical costs
> + admin costs
> + profits
> = premiums.

requiring enough policyholders to spread the risks. The business case set coverage limits.

No health insurance company can survive or provide coverage for anyone if the only people who buy policies are those who require medical care. Similarly, no auto insurance company can survive selling policies only to people with poor driving records and have had lots of accidents.

Such fiscal pragmatism is the basis of the ACA requirement that everyone must purchase coverage. As the "individual mandate" fell under the Trump administration, health insurance companies felt compelled to raise premiums to remain viable.

Health insurance emulates property insurance on deductibles, so it set limits or caps before care services would be covered, like caps on the coverage for homeowners and auto insurance. Lifetime caps or limits on health insurance of $250,000, $500,000 and $1 million were not uncommon. The ACA banned lifetime caps and limits. Insurance companies now must pay all these claims without any end in sight. This stresses their business viability.

Before the ACA, deductibles were a disincentive to preventative care. The ACA requires insurance companies to cover preventive care services without a copayment or coinsurance, even if a patient has not met the annual deductible. The rule requires an outlay by health insurance companies, but since the individual mandate was repealed, the risk can't be spread out among many anymore .

You may or may not agree with the individual mandate, but in practical terms, its repeal has added to the reasons health insurance companies are raising premiums to stay in business.

Insurance Funds Medical Advances

Health insurance, for all its criticisms, should be complimented for dramatic improvements in the sophistication of health services. All those dollars paid by insurance companies become the income for health care providers. Health insurance let medical caregivers end their dependency on charity, replacing pleas for donations with a dependable source of funding.

Reliable funding from health insurance has been a stimulus for expanding medical research and transferring research to practical use. Reliable funding allows medical device makers, pharmaceutical companies, and research hospitals to develop new lifesaving medical technologies that otherwise would lack funding.

Consider the 1972 expansion to Medicare, which covered those suffering End State Renal Disease (ESRD) kidney failure. Before then, there was limited investment in dialysis machines and services, mostly at the academic medical centers. Limited time allocations were decided by committees that selected who would receive life-continuing treatments. Access to funds meant access to care.

> Reliable funding from insurance has been a stimulus for expanding medical research.

Due to Medicare expansion, more patients with ESRD began to survive. The U.S. Renal Data System in 2016 reported close to 350,000 people having a primary diagnosis of renal failure. In 2013, Medicare reported its costs for treating patients with chronic kidney disease (CKD) surpassed $50 billion — 20 percent of all the Medicare spending for those over 65 years old.

Patients surviving renal failure live with other chronic diseases. Between 2010 and 2013, Medicare patients with chronic conditions accounted for $8 billion of the total $9 billion in Medicare spending growth. Seventy percent of Medicare spending for CKD patients over age 65 had diabetes, congestive heart failure, or both.

Health insurance has funded medical advancements, yet these have come with a significant advance in costs.

Early History of Health Insurance

If health care costs are now routine, expected and predictable, then a financing model designed for a rare event is not a model for successfully financing healthcare nor for improving the health status of Americans. How did we land in our current circumstances?

Is there an evil cabal pulling the strings? Or, is there a series of unfortunate decisions and non-decisions, coupled with ideology?

The USA is the only "industrialized" or "first world" country without a national health care plan — some model of nationalized coverage. How we historically got into this situation is the lack of national leadership, coupled with competing ideas of individual responsibility versus collective responsibility.

In early America, individual health was an individual and family responsibility. There were few medical interventions, and these were not costly. Birth was at home, often attended by older women from the community. "Preventive care" meant "an apple a day keeps the doctor away." No immunizations. No cancer screening. If you got sick, you recovered or died without costly interventions.

As cities grew, people living in close quarters raised concerns of communicable diseases. In port cities, efforts were made to stop sailors or immigrants from carrying diseases. Early hospitals cared for those without families and quarantined those with identifiably communicable illnesses. Medical care, if available, cost little.

Before widespread immunization, for example, tuberculosis (TB) ravaged the urban poor in the late 19th and early 20th centuries. The response was to build TB sanitariums in rural areas.

Immigrants from the "old country" formed associations to help each other in the new one. Early "benevolent" associations, such as the fraternal order of Elks and Foresters, early credit unions, and burial societies, often served ethnic or religious communities. Regular payments by all members funded payments to any member who became ill or injured.

> Payments by all members of a 'benevolent' association funded the payments to any member who became ill or injured.

Commercial insurance started before the Civil War to provide coverage for injuries related to travel by railroad or steamboat. Massachusetts Health Insurance in Boston offered an early group insurance policy in 1847.

As America industrialized, employers began to pay for the health care of employees and the families of employees. Their motivation: You can't run a factory if your employees are out sick. "Company towns" offered company physicians and clinics. Otto von Bismarck in 1884 mandated health coverage for all Germans from the same motive: A strong military requires a healthy population.

Health insurance got its real start during the Great Depression. With fewer patients able to pay, and those with jobs facing hardship if they became ill, hospitals began to offer insurance for the costs of hospital care. A network of local insurance companies united as the Blue Cross, based on a 1920s offer by Baylor University Hospital to

Dallas public school teachers. Baylor provided hospital services to teachers for 50 cents a month. Physician charges were not included, so physicians formed the national Blue Shield in 1939. The separate federations, Blue Cross and Blue Shield, merged in 1982.

The Great Depression sparked commercial health insurance, and World War II spawned employer-sponsored health insurance.

Military conscription created labor shortages, yet factories had to increase their labor force to meet wartime production. Government wage controls limited the ability to offer higher wages, so factories turned to fringe benefits for attracting workers. Health benefits, the more generous the better, became a major recruitment tool.

Employer-sponsored health insurance got a boost in 1943 when the Internal Revenue Service ruled that the cost of health insurance, if provided through an employer, was tax-free to the employee and tax-deductible for the employer. This tax advantage for employer-sponsored health insurance was reconfirmed in 1954.

Nine percent of the population was covered by voluntary private health insurance in 1940, growing to 63 percent by 1953 and then 70 percent in the 1960s, according to an NPR "Planet Money" report. Private health insurance seemed to be working for America.

Advent of Medicare and Medicaid

Two dark clouds hovered over private health insurance from both not-for-profit insurers like Blue Cross and Blue Shield and the commercial for-profit companies like Aetna. The poor people not in the workforce, and those who aged out of the workforce, the elderly over age 65, were not being covered by health insurance.

Medical care had extended people's lives beyond their working years, yet older people were being impoverished by health care costs. The poor and unemployed, relegated to charity services, were being squeezed by the costs of medical advances.

Americans don't like the idea of people dying on the street, or seeing their parents, who spent a lifetime working, retire into abject poverty brought on by health care costs. Something had to be done. The government responded in 1960 with the Kerr-Mills Act to match state funds to cover patients' bills, but that was not enough.

After extensive wrangling, as part of President Lyndon Johnson's Great Society, Congress in 1965 enacted Medicare for people over age 65 and Medicaid for the poor.

Medicare's fiscal model is based on insurance, funded during a person's worklife by payroll deductions and employer contributions. Medicaid is funded by federal taxes, allocated based on state poverty levels, plus state and local taxes. The state controls Medicaid benefit levels. Local counties control individual enrollments.

Health insurance companies did not oppose Medicaid, for poor people were not potential customers. For the medical community, especially for hospitals, Medicaid meant more reliable money than was possible from charity.

Physicians were different. Many physicians had willingly provided care to their poor patients without compensation, so now they could be paid. However, a bureaucracy now intervened in what physicians saw as their moral duty. Changing the physicians' moral duty into a commercial transaction shifted the focus from healing to business. Some physicians refused Medicaid participation and yet still provided unpaid health care to the poor.

> Changing physicians' moral duty to a commercial transaction shifted the focus from healing to business.

Medicare, in contrast, was initially opposed by the commercial insurance industry, then logic prevailed. People work until age 65 and retire in relative health. When their big medical bills roll in, they are no longer on private insurance, so no loss of profits!

The medical community itself was harder to convince. Medicare could be a boon to physicians' incomes since patients needing their services now had a reliable funding source. Initially, services were virtually unconstrained, and payment reflected a high percentage of customary medical fees. The medical community's enthusiasm then was dampened by the potential of government, a third party, taking a greater role, influencing or commanding care activities, impacting the physician-patient relationship.

Here was the vision: Employer-sponsored health insurance for the workers, Medicare for the elderly. Medicaid for the poor. Gaps in coverage from unemployment were handled by the Consolidated Omnibus Budget Reconciliation Act (COBRA), enabling individuals to extend employer-sponsored health insurance up to 18 months, paying the premiums themselves until they found another job.

Virtually everyone was covered. What could go wrong?

What Went Wrong

In theory, all was right with the world. What went wrong was cost emulating the New York State motto, *excelsior*, ever upward.

Health care costs grew from a nominal expenditure by employers and taxpayers into expenditures sucking up more and more dollars. The Centers for Disease Control reported health care costs in 1960 were $26 billion, 5.2 percent of the Gross Domestic Product (GDP). Costs by 1990 reached $725 billion at 12.4 percent of GDP, and they are projected to reach $5 trillion by 2020 at 20 percent of GDP.

Meanwhile, worker's compensation insurance reduces take-home pay, and so do increased Medicare payroll deductions. Medicaid keeps pushing up federal, state and local taxes. The health insurance model worked until the costs of providing care drove premiums and tax support to the point of pain.

The new gold mine of health insurance financed physicians, hospitals, pharmaceutical firms, medical device manufacturers, and care providers of all types. As new and improved services rushed to meet ever-growing patient needs, costs continued to grow.

> The insurance model worked until the costs of care drove premiums and taxes to the point of pain.

Hospitals had to purchase the very latest diagnostic equipment. Radiology offered a CT scanner and then an MRI. By 2016, the USA had nearly 37 MRI machines for each million people, according to Statista. Canada had nine MRIs for each million people. All of this hiked hospital costs.

The payment model for health care services was both simple and inflationary. Policyholders accepted whatever services the medical community offered, each effective and medically necessary, and the insurance would cover the costs up to the policy limits. Those limits were generous, a high percentage of "usual and customary" charges. U&C charges skyrocketed. As long as physicians agreed to accept insurance payments in full, patients willingly played along.

Health insurance paid for it all, virtually without any question. Multiple visits for the same condition, even hospitalization for the convenience of a family, such as admitting Mom so children could go on vacation. Effectiveness was not tracked, nor was quality. If some medical error required hospital re-admission, health insurance paid the bill without question. Happy days in healthcare.

As the cost of healthcare rose, so did health insurance premiums, so did Medicare premiums, and so did taxes to support Medicaid. The easy focus was — and to a large degree remains — on the cost of health insurance, Medicare, and what taxpayers pay for Medicaid. The real culprit is the cost of medical services. As costs grew, so did the schemes and plans to constrain them.

States stepped in to limit the "unit costs" of services provided to Medicaid recipients. Medicare created a schedule of allowable fees. Commercial insurance passed on cost increases to the employers, who often passed them to employees as increased payroll deductions. Hospitals in many states came under laws that tried to control the rates they charged. Medicare moved from payments based on length of hospital stay to payments based on diagnosis.

Commercial plans reduced premiums by reducing benefits, such as not covering physician visits unless the patient had an illness (so much for preventive care) increasing co-pays at the time of service, and by tightening underwriting on who they would insure.

Managed Care

The most impactful scheme to "bend the cost curve," to restrain the rate of cost growth, was a model that Henry Kaiser developed during construction of the Hoover Dam, later used in the shipyard where Liberty ships were mass-produced during World War II.

The "managed care" model of health maintenance organizations, HMOs, approached costs, quality and bureaucracy differently.

The original Kaiser model became the Kaiser Permanente Health Plan. It called for the insurer to control the medical delivery system, to manage individuals' care throughout the system, eliminate waste and duplication, monitor quality, and implement treatment plans that prove to be the most effective for the least cost. As a result, the cost to the patient and to the employer could be constrained.

The goal of managed care was to serve the long-term interests of patients' health. Offer them easy access to a primary care physician, so patients saw physicians early in an illness. Early interventions lowered costs. Benefits were enhanced. Lifetime caps were removed. By owning a system of hospitals, outpatient services and physicians, HMOs were motivated to provide care in the least costly setting.

The one fly in the medicinal ointment? Patients were required to use only the HMO's system, its hospitals and physicians. Channeling or corralling Americans into such a system met with resistance.

President Richard Nixon in 1973 signed the Health Maintenance Organization Act, known as the Federal HMO Act. Sen. Edward M. Kennedy was the principal sponsor.

HMOs took off. What started as a movement expected to enroll 20 percent of the population has become the universal model for delivering coverage, not only for employer-sponsored health plans, but also for Medicare and Medicaid. HMOs were able, initially, to put the brakes on costs, chiefly unit costs, as they contracted with medical providers and hospitals at discounted rates.

> As HMOs moved past controlling costs to managing care, sparks began to fly.

Just as physicians had feared with the advent of Medicare, adding a third party to the patient-physician relationship affected that relationship. As HMOs moved past controlling unit costs to actually managing care, sparks began to fly.

Patients did not want to stay restricted to the HMO's network, and they did not want to go get permission to go see a specialist. Medical providers did not want to be told to whom they could refer patients, nor to be pressured to use alternatives to traditional treatment plans, such as outpatient care. Horror stories told of patients limited to "in network" coverage and deficient access to quality care by in-network providers.

Although much went wrong with HMOs, much went right, too. For a period of time, cost increases stabilized. However, the initial HMO strategy could not hold down costs long term.

Market resentment toward "managed care" (by both patients and physicians) doomed the underlying model. Over time, inflationary fee-for-service models returned as the norm.

The Affordable Care Act

Health insurance premiums kept increasing by double digits, two to three times the rate of inflation. Employers balanced the costs by passing along rate increases through higher payroll deductions and fewer wage increases. States grappled with Medicaid costs by cutting fees paid for Medicaid services. Medicare restrained costs by cutting hospital rates and limiting increases in physician fees.

As premiums rose, insurance companies dug back into their bag of tricks to slow rate increases. Individual and small group policies became either unavailable or unaffordable. Small businesses gave up and dropped coverage completely.

The Great Recession of 2008 became the great disrupter in health insurance. The ensuing reform, the Affordable Care Act, proudly or derisively called Obamacare, changed health insurance dramatically while changing the structure of care delivery.

The concept is simple. Get 100 percent of the U.S. population insured. With everyone insured, every citizen would have coverage, forever removing economics as a barrier to healthcare services. All would be protected from financial devastation for necessary care. Wisely, the cost of delivering care would be spread over the entire population by mandate, in effect nationalizing the cost of medical care but not the delivery of care. No exclusions for preexisting conditions. No lifetime caps. No longer would affordable health care insurance be available only through an employer.

Under the ACA, hospitals, doctors and other caregivers would no longer carry the load of providing services without payment, uncompensated care, passing on the costs to others.

Don't force people into one plan. Let them choose from among comparable plans. Let them pick a plan based on price, reputation and the plan's included providers, hospitals and physicians. Keep confusion out of plan selection by mandating four benefit packages, labeled as Bronze, Silver, Gold, and Platinum.

For those of low income, expand Medicaid coverage by bringing Medicaid insurance to those with incomes up to 132 percent of the Federal Poverty Level. For those of modest means, subsidize the purchase of "approved" insurance plans, available to those between 133 and 400 percent of the Federal Poverty Level.

> The ACA's promises were more political than practical.

The ACA's promises were more political than practical.

President Obama's promise — "If you like your doctor, you can keep your doctor." — should have included a qualifying asterisk. The ability to keep your doctor depended on whether or not your physician chose (or was chosen) to participate in a plan "approved" under the ACA. Turned out that expanding Medicaid eligibility did not expand the number of participating physicians.

For approved plans with standard benefits under metallic labels, differences rested on price and network — the medical community contracted to provide care under the insurance policy.

Narrow Care Networks

The products offered through a Health Insurance Exchange do not cover out-of-network care except in an emergency, which often means no coverage. These "narrow" networks are claustrophobic.

Each insurance carrier uses propriety data, propriety algorithms, to decide which providers can be in its narrow network. This lacks transparency and disregards existing patient-physician relationships. Is cost the only criteria? What about quality or efficiency?

For example, Empire BlueCross BlueShield created the narrow "Pathways" network for its 2014 offering by excluding all academic medical centers in New York City, such as Sloan Kettering, plus all the physicians associated with those institutions. For 2015, Empire broadened that network, but it could shrink in the future. The only insurer offering products on New Hampshire's exchange, Anthem (BlueCross BlueShield) excluded ten of the state's 26 hospitals. Hospitals are included or excluded based on unit price.

These narrow networks often are state-specific. You can't cross state lines for covered care, even if your insurance company sells the product in every state. This may not be known until care is needed, or after it's obtained, increasing the patient's economic risk.

Who fits in these "chosen" networks is a source of confusion and mystery to patients and physicians alike. Health plans do not make it easy. Network and product names constantly change, and so do the rules for participating physicians.

UnitedHealthcare has products called Core, Metro and Charter. Physicians participating in the networks called Freedom and Liberty do not participate in these products unless a patient is in a hospital, and if the physician is participating. How is a physician or a patient to keep this nuance clear? Patients get caught in the confusion.

Verifying if your physician is in a narrow network is a challenge in itself. Reviews of the online directories by the health plans have revealed high degrees of inaccuracy, such as the lack of availability of the listed physicians, who are not accepting new patients. The Los Angeles Times in 2014 reported that 12.8 percent of the physicians in Anthem's online directory for California were not accepting new patients, and 25 percent of the office locations were inaccurate.

'You Can Keep Your Current Plan'

"If you like your current health insurance plan, you can keep it." This politic statement also needs an asterisk. Yes, you can keep your plan, but only if it meets federal requirements.

The ACA set up essential benefits that all health insurance plans must cover. If your current health insurance plan did not include all these essential benefits, it was not approved under the ACA.

Non-conforming policies get labeled as "junk policies" because of large gaps in the health benefits. Junk policies do satisfy the needs and desires of some younger and healthier purchasers, who care about affordability more than benefits. A single male does not need maternity benefits, for instance, so 66 percent of male purchasers chose that cost savings, according to Healthcare.org.

However, limitations in junk policies often are discovered only when the excluded care is most needed, creating economic burdens for patients causing medical debt for their caregivers.

In fairness to the ACA, it makes sense to set minimum standards on what must be covered under a health insurance policy.

The Trump administration policy allows states to approve non-conforming policies, those with less coverage and lower premiums. Excluding coverage for mental health, substance abuse treatment or maternity care does reduce premiums. Why pay a higher premium for services you do not expect to use? However, short-term savings on premiums may be regretted long-term when superior coverage is needed. One needs to balance costs and risks.

Metallic Plans and Medical Debt

More than half of the personal bankruptcies in this nation relate to medical bills and the economic stress on families and individuals by the cost of care. The ACA was designed to address this tragedy, but does it really solve the problem?

Bronze, Silver, Gold, and Platinum insurance plans. Not all that glitters is good. Each of these metallic labels carries a different level of patient financial responsibility. None of these coverage categories offer full protection from medical debt and financial ruin.

Healthpocket.com explains the situation. Bronze plans with the most affordable premiums cover only 60 percent of the care costs, leaving 40 percent of the responsibly on patients and families. Bronze plans have a $3,000 deductible for individuals and $6,000 for families. The out-of-pocket cap is $6,350 for individuals and $12,700 for families. Gold plans, in contrast, cover 70 percent of the costs with a $2,000 deductible for individuals and $4,000 for families, plus a $5,500 out-of-pocket maximum for individuals and $11,000 for families. Clearly, those of modest means risk personal or family economic devastation.

> Bronze, Silver, Gold, and Platinum insurance plans. Not all that glitters is good.

Patient's financial responsibility is not eliminated by ACA. The public may be lulled into a false sense of security. Those deductibles are hefty, adding to cost-sharing by the healthcare providers like physicians and hospitals. As the patient's financial responsibility for a claim goes up, so does the provider's risk and likelihood of non-payment. Medical debt remains a big problem for all.

Patient's eligibility is not guaranteed. Even if a provider verifies coverage at the time of care, individuals who purchase coverage on an exchange are given a grace period to pay their monthly insurance premium. Care providers will receive a confirmation the patient is covered even if a premium remains unpaid up to 90 days after it was due. About 20 percent of those buying individual policies on health exchanges default before the end of their grace period.

The ACA removed barriers to buying health insurance, removed bans on preexisting conditions, provided coverage for children up to age 26 under a family plan, made coverage available to individuals without employer-provided plans, and expanded the availability of Medicaid. All of this, along with premium subsidies, increased affordability for a large segment of the middle class.

The result has been a clear decrease in the number of uninsured. According to Kaiser Family Foundation research, the number of uninsured non-elderly Americans decreased from 44 million in 2013 (the year before ACA coverage provisions took effect) to fewer than 28 million uninsured at the end of 2016.

The same Kaiser report warns that the affordability of insurance policies remains an issue. High costs are the principal reason most often cited by those who remain uninsured.

The ACA Is Really Insurance Reform

One of the key provisions of the ACA converted health insurance companies into public utilities, and so regulated their profitability. Insurance products must pay out 85 percent (80 percent for a small group policy) for medical services, leaving 15 to 20 percent for both administration and profitability. Spending more on medical clams, insurance companies adsorb the loss, spend less, and must refund the difference to the policyholders. Profitability is not what it once was for insurance companies.

The cost of health insurance is still tied to the cost of care — unit cost and the volume of services. There's been little impact here.

From 2008 to 2016, health plan costs rose by 50 percent, reflected in the higher insurance premiums paid by employers and the higher payroll deductions of employees.

Employers offset the increases by applying the deductible models of the ACA marketplace plans. If anything, the ACA legitimized and reintroduced the deductible as a major tool for shifting the cost of care to the patient. By 2016, Money magazine reports, deductibles above $1,000 were standard, and 51 percent of insured employees were exposed to high out-of-pocket costs.

> ACA did little to change the fundamental structure for the delivery of health care.

The ACA did little to change the fundamental structure for the delivery of health care. It did not move hospitals to communities where most needed, increase the supply of primary care physicians, increase ambulatory care options, nor end medical debt.

The necessary re-engineering of care delivery has been left to the healthcare industry, which has proven itself to be more dedicated to protecting the status quo and their bottom line than in adopting reforms that meet evolving community medical needs.

I believe that insurance is the wrong way to finance healthcare. We cannot end medical debt without addressing the core structures driving high health care costs. We need to rethink our approach.

*I attribute my success to this:
I never gave or took any excuse.*
— Florence Nightingale

CHAPTER 8

No Thank You For Your Service

Jerry Ashton

Writing this chapter was difficult for me. It was difficult to write without getting angry. I'll tell you why.

On November 11, 2017, for the first time in more than 50 years, I put back on my old Navy uniform to march in the New York City Veterans Day Parade. I was joined by Mikel Burroughs, retired Army colonel, and Hutch Dubosque, a Vietnam-era Army sergeant. We're there for RIP at America's largest annual Veterans Day parade.

As I marched in uniform that day (amazed it still fits), someone called out, "Thank you for your service!" I appreciated and accepted acknowledgement of the years I served many decades ago as a Navy journalist. Even so, I heard those words with mixed emotions.

I felt compelled to write a blog about the experience, suggesting that we replace the words, "Thank you for your service," with action. This was my polite way to request that the person shaking my hand express a more useful form of gratitude. I provided a way this might be done — forgive veterans' medical debt! I touched a nerve.

Back in 2014, after Craig Antico and I first founded RIP as a tax-deductible way for any American to help us locate, buy and forgive medical debt, we realized helping hard-pressed people in the general population was not enough. As donations came in and we purchased debt, we noticed a surprising percentage of the medical bills forgiven were from veterans and active-duty military. That's off.

We realized that RIP must be anchored in two different worlds, both debt buying and military charities. A referral led me to Mikel Burroughs. Perfect fit. Mikel (say like "Michael") served as an Army brigade commander in Kuwait and Iraq. Retired as a bird colonel, Mikel is a veteran C-suite collections industry executive who's bought and sold billions in medical debt. He rides a Harley and likes to drum. He's active on RallyPoint for vets.

Mikel felt as ardently about forgiving veterans' medical debt as do Craig and I. We began a campaign, #NoVetMedDebt, that's been crucial in reaching our 2018 goal of forgiving $50 million in veterans' medical debt. Our efforts barely scratch the surface.

Vets Do Have Medical Debt

You may be asking, how can any men and women in the service, (active-duty or veterans), have medical debt? What about Veterans Affairs (VA) and the Veterans Benefits Administration?

Like most Americans (including myself as a veteran), I believed our country fully covers the medical needs of men and women who serve our country. Many return from deployments suffering severe disabilities, visible or not. Our nation would and should care for our warriors as a patriotic way of showing our thanks, right?

When entering the military, men and women sign a blank check, saying, "I'm yours to use as needed, America, up to and including my death." Year after year, America cashes that check. So, of course, we take care of all our troops in return. Certainly, we do!

I've learned it's not quite that way, not in every case. Consider the regs and hoops a vet must jump through to get medical care at the VA. Consider VA refusals to cover vets for off-site care by non-military physicians, clinics and hospitals, or for emergency transport. "Uncle Sugar" does not cover everything. Millions, no, billions of dollars in medical bills are landing on the backs of our veterans.

> Billions in medical debt are landing on the backs of our veterans.

Consider our veterans' vital statistics: About 20 veterans a day commit suicide. More than 50,000 homeless vets seek shelter nightly. More than 50 percent of returning vets suffer from PTSD. Many vets discover their long-term health care needs outlast their Veterans Affairs benefits. In 2010, roughly 1.3 million uninsured veterans had out-of-pocket medical costs beyond their disposable income.

As evidence of the scale, Paige Kutilek at GoFundMe says the site hosts campaigns by tens of thousands of military veterans plagued with unpaid medical debt. Bill collectors hound them.

Medical debt is no way to thank those who risked their lives.

Hard reality is why RIP decided early to forgive veterans' debt as our special focus. This was a development I did not expect, not even as a Navy sailor. I still thought, isn't our government supposed to be responsible for all who serve, who have served, all who sacrifice for our country? We surely do right by them, yes? Not quite, not nearly well enough, I've learned, and sometimes not at all.

From buying and forgiving veterans' debt, I have identified ways the VA (which is you and me) evades or avoids its responsibilities to veterans. I'll offer three varied examples of the situation.

The Case of 'Veteran Alpha'

We were contacted for debt relief by a 73-year-old Army veteran ("Veteran Alpha") unable to pay his high medical bills. On Veterans Day 2016, Veteran Alpha visited his ailing wife at the local hospital. While there, he suffered a cardiac arrest and underwent emergency heart bypass surgery. Before the surgery, the hospital duly advised the area's largest VA medical center about his precarious condition. They wanted to send an ambulance from 75 miles away to transport him back to the VA for any further care.

The hospital staff put Alpha on the phone with the VA center. He groggily told the VA person that he already was being prepped for surgery, and he wasn't going to wait for them. His life was at risk. He ended the call and went into surgery. He survived.

After his surgery, Alpha was swamped with medical bills the VA declined to pay because he had "refused emergency transport."

The hospital surgery bill was $180,000. Medicare paid about 80 percent. The hospital pursued the $35,000 balance. Alpha emptied a $7,000 savings account and borrowed $7,000 from the Navy Federal Credit Union. This left the married couple with $15,000 still due to the hospital. Alpha depended upon regular federal payments for his service-related 100 percent disability. Adding monthly loan payments atop household costs, plus pittances to the hospital, had put Alpha and his wife in jeopardy of losing their home.

Liver Fluke Cancer and the VA

Hutch DuBosque has been waging a fight to secure VA coverage for a rare bile duct cancer and liver disease caused by the parasite, *Platyhelminthes*. Several of Hutch's Vietnam-era vet friends came down with a "weird disease" from an obscure parasite called a "liver fluke." Before two of them passed, Hutch and his crew promised their dying friends to research this disease and save others' lives.

The river fluke, according to the American Cancer Society, is a freshwater-borne flatworm found in military men and women who served in eastern and southeastern Asia. It produces a protein called "granulum," which is highly carcinogenic, basically a death sentence. If caught in its dormancy, the parasite is treatable. If not discovered, it inevitably presents Stage 4 cancer in the pancreas or liver.

Hutch insists the VA resists covering treatment for the parasite, denying claims by arguing, "It's not been proven."

> The VA denied claims, arguing, 'It's not been proven.'

Hutch and four of his friends (John Ball, Gerry Wiggins, Larry Noon, and Ralph Goodwin) volunteered for a 50-person pilot study by the VA Medical Center at Northport, NY. Veterans who reported eating undercooked freshwater fish while in Vietnam donated blood samples for serological exam at Seoul National University College of Medicine in South Korea. The blood went there since no U.S. facility can reliably identify the antigen marker of the Asian parasite.

The January 2018 issue of Infectious Diseases in Clinical Practice published Norfolk's study report, "Screening U.S. Vietnam Veterans for Liver Fluke Exposure 5 Decades After the End of the War."

Hutch and his friends were interviewed by their area newspaper, Newsday, for a story about the Long Island study. The VA found almost one in four of the 50 Vietnam veterans harbored the parasite, which can live dormant in a body for decades, Newsday reported. One in four of the study group tested positive for bile duct cancer. Since 2013, Newsday said, the VA had received 240 claims for bile duct cancers attributed to the liver fluke, and the VA had "rejected more than 76 percent of those claims."

Hutch says, "This disease is three times as big as Agent Orange, but its victims are systematically being denied disability claims by the VA." Three million GIs served in Vietnam. More serve today in the parasite's range, including South Korea. Neither the VA nor the Department of Defense routinely screens for the parasite.

The five Long Island veterans next reached out to Sen. Chuck Schumer (D-NY) and Rep. Tom Suozzi (D-NY), who then released statements calling for a broader study.

The Department of Veterans Affairs initiated a mortality study of Vietnam-era vets going back 60 years to determine any connection between parasite exposure and liver bile cancer. However, Newsday said, the announcement has done little to calm nerves.

Hutch's buddy, Gerald Wiggins, tested positive for bile cancer. In 2018 he had cancerous cysts removed from his liver at Memorial Sloan Kettering Cancer Center. He'll return every year for a new CT scan, but he's unsure how to pay for any further care.

"Friends are dying," Wiggins complained, "but no one at the VA can give us any direct answers on what's going on with disease coverage, if they are going to treat us, so we can live. The VA dances around this whole thing while vets get more medical bills."

For me, his story conveys, "No thank you for your service."

Burn Pit Veterans

This one was new to me, discovered only when RIP received this one veteran's request for help at our website.

"I realize that you buy bundles of old debt, so debt forgiveness is random, and you can't help individuals. But us burn pit veterans get short shrift. We don't get real help from the VA. I have not found a fund that helps burn pit veterans afford medications or inhalers or oxygen to benefit their daily living."

Burn pits? What in blazes are they? I began doing research.

The VA dances around while vets get more medical bills.

The Department of Veterans Affairs defines a "burn pit" as the common way the military got rid of its waste at military sites in the Middle East war zones. They burned chemicals, paint, medical and human waste, munitions, and unexploded ordinance — just about everything combustible went into a burn pit, fouling the air.

In response to growing concerns from mounting evidence that military personnel and contractors who worked at or near "burn pits" were suffering from excessive lung diseases, in June 2014, the VA launched the "Airborne Hazards and Open Burn Pit Registry." Had the registry made a difference for burn pit veterans?

A referral led me to the D.C. offices of U.S. Rep. Raul Ruiz (D-CA), himself a physician. "Burn pits absolutely are a major concern," he declared, "and I'm doing something about it."

Dr. Ruiz in 2018 launched the bipartisan Congressional Burn Pits Caucus with Brad Wenstrup, GOP chair of the House Veterans' Affairs subcommittee with 21 bipartisan members. The "Helping Veterans Exposed to Burn Pits Act" became law in September 2018. The bill directs the Department of Veterans Affairs to establish a center of excellence in the prevention, diagnosis, mitigation, treatment, and rehabilitation of health conditions relating to exposure to burn pits or other environmental exposures in Afghanistan or Iraq.

Now that's real help! Thank you for your service.

After Veterans Day, What?

The 20 million men and women alive today who have served a grateful nation deserve attention. After Veterans Day, after the flags are furled, after the marching bands return home, then what?

If you are akin to many Americans, you take time each Veterans Day to honor those who have fought and still fight for our country. Perhaps you stand to watch or join a parade in the smallest towns to the largest cities across the country.

More probably, you only watch a parade snippet on the evening news, perhaps after visiting the shopping mall to take advantage of "Veterans Day Bargains!" Sadder still, maybe the day passed without you ever noticing or giving vets any thought.

The attention paid to veterans tends to fade after Veterans Day. Vets starve for attention the other 364 days of the year. The parades are over. The cemetery salutes are done. The vets we thank for their service are still here, and too often they are underserved.

Veterans' Medical Debt

Among the segments of American society most indebted by our healthcare system, the military and veterans stand out.

Herb Weisbaum at NBC News covered the Consumer Financial Protection Bureau (renamed by Acting Director Mick Mulvaney as the Bureau of Consumer Financial Protection). Half the complaints received from service members in 2015, Weisbaum reported, dealt with debt collectors. Veterans also file twice the level of complaints as does the general public.

NBC News said that military members and veterans "report being hounded to pay medical bills that should have been covered by insurance" (e.g., the VA, Medicare, Medicaid, and private).

Military members are easily pressured by bill collectors to pay a bill (even if not owed or not

> **Veterans with medical debt are stones squeezing out blood.**

correct) for fear a collection agency may (illegally) contact their commanding officer, hurting a military career, or (legally) place a bad mark on a credit report, hurting their financial recovery. They may dread the stress, perhaps knowing it may harm their health.

To our shame as a nation, in my eyes, a large part of our veterans' burden comes in the form of medical debt. No matter what they do or say to each collection agency, they are stones squeezing out blood. The calls and letters never stop. This is why RIP makes a special effort to forgive veterans' medical debt, such as abolishing more than $50 million in vet debt in 2018 alone. We thank the allies joining forces with us in a priority emergency mission to complete with honor.

Veterans' Unemployment

Sen. Bob Casey (D-CA), a ranking Finance Committee member, reported that, on average, 30 percent of all returning vets aged 18-24 are unprepared for the road ahead, not ready for the struggles with personal finances, low-paying jobs, and unemployment. Regardless of their willingness to protect their families, they lack the experience and resources to handle serious financial adversity.

Almost 50 percent of the 20 million U.S. veterans participate in the labor force. So, more than 10 million veterans are not working or not actively looking for work. Some veterans give up on ever finding a job. Some veterans are retired or on disability. Some may be in school. There are many reasons for not being in the labor force.

We have 9.9 million employed veterans, reported the U.S. Bureau of Labor Statistics in 2017.

Nearly one third of all working vets are deemed underemployed, according to ZipRecruiter as well as the Call of Duty Endowment, which helps veterans find jobs.

Millions of vets hold jobs they are overqualified to do. They risk their lives for our country, and we do not value their skills.

Homeless Veterans

Due to poverty and inadequate support networks, 1.4 million veterans risk homelessness, reported the VFW Magazine. An Iraq war member helping homeless veterans in Missouri told the magazine, "I was leaving as many vets on the streets as I was helping. They took the oath just like me. Why am I treated better?"

Few homeless vets qualify for VA help. Too many such vets are being told "no." They haven't served long enough, for instance, or they don't qualify for VA benefits after getting in legal trouble, like a DUI, in which case all VA benefits may be taken away.

Military Times in 2017 reported the number of homeless vets has risen for the first time in seven years. Some 50,000 sleep in shelters nightly across America. The story cited VA Secretary David Shulkin admitting that "zero homeless veterans" is not a realistic target.

Veterans' Suicides

The U.S. Department of Veterans Affairs (VA) released findings from its most recent analysis of veteran suicide data for all 50 states and the District of Columbia.

This report yields several important insights:

• Suicide rates increased for both veterans and non-veterans, underscoring that suicide is a national public health concern.

• The average number of veterans who died by suicide each day remained unchanged at 20.

• The suicide rate increased faster among the veterans who had little used the Veterans Health Administration care plan, compared to those who had sought coverage.

(For the full analysis, see the "VA National Suicide Data Report 2005-2015." Based on 55 million civilian and veteran death records, the report grounds the VA's Suicide Prevention Program.)

Any part medical debt plays in veterans' suicides is too much.

Charity for Veterans

GrantSpace estimates 1.5 million nonprofit organizations in the USA. GuideStar estimates 45,000 nonprofits devoted to veterans and their families. Did you know only 18 percent of these are 501(c)(3) charities that can accept tax-deductible contributions?

These organizations come in every stripe and color, according to a CNBC report on the "Top 10 Charities That Support Veterans." Some were formed by military wives or focus on specific branches of service. One charity, Puppies Behind Bars, trains prison inmates to raise service dogs for wounded war veterans.

The organizations most Americans might recognize include the Veterans of Foreign Wars (VFW) and Disabled American Veterans (DAV). A relative newcomer is Wounded Warriors, begun 2003 in Roanoke by a group of Virginia veterans and their friends who chose to take action to help injured service men and women.

We can tell you from experience that Americans are incredibly giving once they're aware of a need deserving attention. RIP met our 2018 goal to abolish $50 million in veteran debt in a #NoVetMedDebt campaign. Next year, we're shooting for $100 million.

RIP is able to help any organization — military or civilian — raise funds to abolish unpaid and unpayable medical bills for military and veterans. As a way to say, "Thank you for your service," let's commit to leaving no man or woman behind.

*A billion here, a billion there,
sooner or later it adds up to real money.*

— Everett Dirksen

CHAPTER 9

Health Is a Goal, Not an Industry

Robert Goff

We Americans have an odd concept of healthcare. We will not tolerate people being deprived of it, yet we just don't want to pay for someone else's care. Services essential to a whole community must be paid for by each individual. This results in medical debt for individuals without the resources of insurance or cash.

We debate who should pick up the tab, missing the reality that we all pay for healthcare for everyone. Each of us picks up the tab for the health insurance plan premiums, payroll deductions for premiums, deductions for Medicare, taxes for Medicaid, and taxes to subsidize the deficits of hospitals and clinics that aren't making it financially. Each of us are paying for the losses and consequences of sickness in public disability payments, public support of medically impoverished families, and economic losses from lost job productivity.

The $3 trillion healthcare spending tab in the USA is about sick care, about accident care, health restoration. It is about the business of providing care, which is not the true business of health.

Shouldn't the discussion or debate be far wider?

Shouldn't we be as concerned, or more concerned, about health itself? How can the health status of Americans be lifted? If we'd focus on health not costs, I propose, the costs of care would be positively impacted, stabilized or reduced. Acting to prevent or mitigate illness or injury is not widely seen as the mission of health care. Meanwhile, our health costs keep going up. This defies reason.

> Acting to prevent or mitigate illness or injury is not widely seen as the mission of health care.

In my ideal, a health system concerned with patient health would better influence the trajectory of needed care. Utilization of medical services would be decided using a *failure analysis model* to determine the causes of health issues and implement corrective actions. When a patient requires a higher-cost, more intensive service, that would be taken as a "failure to intervene" earlier with lower-cost, less intensive services. Pay a little now to avoid paying more later.

Too little effort is made to avoid care costs by addressing causes. We know the causes of most illness, but efforts are limited for the interventions that reduce the incidence of illness, reduce costs and improve health outcomes. We know the causes of most injuries, but efforts are limited for the interventions that reduce the incidence of injuries, reduce costs and improve outcomes.

Preventive care helps avoid medical spending. Each intervention forestalls or avoids a later, costlier intervention. A healthcare industry that's paid for delivering care services has no such interest.

The medical care of Americans today is the business of the U.S. healthcare industry. The mission and business of the health industry is treating illnesses and accidents after they occur, not before. The care industry is compensated for the production and delivery of care services, by service units, a silo of sickness and accident care in the health restoration and repair business.

Medical spending should go where it can best improve health. In the trillions spent annually on medical care, consider the scale of all the missed opportunities. A Kaiser Family Foundation study, for instance, identified factors increasing risks of premature death. Ten percent of premature deaths were due to the care provided. Another 20 percent were due to social or environmental factors, 30 percent to genetics, and 40 percent for personal behaviors.

Health research and treatment has advanced. Illnesses that in the past meant a premature death today are livable as chronic conditions, which lead to higher medical costs. Becker's Hospital CFO Report says unhealthy behaviors are largely responsible for chronic illnesses like heart disease, cancer and diabetes, which cause about 70 percent of all deaths in the USA and are the most expensive to treat. No one wants to pay for the unhealthy habits of "the other guy."

Personal Responsibility

Personal responsibility is an ethical or a moral tenet in America. Freedom entails responsibility to better oneself, such as responsibility for one's health. The ideal of *self-reliance* explains pushback against all national healthcare proposals that reduce personal responsibility. People should face the consequences of their choices. If the economic risk from not taking care of oneself is borne by others, says this view, then nothing motivates us to engage in healthy behaviors.

Personal responsibility for health is left to individuals. Illness is widely perceived as a consequence of poor personal behavior, so even premature death is a fitting consequence. I see this as a throwback to the times when poor health was a sign of a failure in individual piety. The righteous are granted health; the sinful are made to suffer.

By this view, if your behavior increases your risk of illness, if you suffer economic harm as a result, so be it. Equating illness with risky behavior falls apart when that illness is the result of factors outside the control of the individual., such as genetic predispositions, birth defects, environmental factors, or social conditions.

Self-preservation really should motivate wise choices, but we may do self-destructive behaviors (such as smoking, drinking, drugs) from societal factors (such as poverty). Many causes of illness can't be addressed by lone individuals (such as water and air pollution). We also can't yet alter our genetics after the fact of our birth.

In the sacred name of personal responsibility, we have shifted the economic cost of health care to patients (such as with deductibles and coverage limits). This yields economic hardship for individuals and families, actually making it harder for people to be responsible for themselves.

> In the name of personal responsibility, we shifted the economic cost of health care to patients, making it harder for people to be responsible for themselves.

Self-Destructive Behaviors

Let's look at unhealthy personal behaviors that drive up the costs of healthcare yet begin outside the healthcare system itself.

Smoking: Smoking-related illness costs society more than $300 billion yearly, says the Centers for Disease Control (CDC), including $170 billion for direct medical care with $5.6 billion for secondhand smoke exposure. Taxes on cigarettes to help reduce consumption are offset by manufacturers' discounts to retailers that lower prices for consumers, with $5.8 billion spent in 2016 to subsidize smoking.

Alcohol: Alcohol abuse costs U.S. society more than $249 billion a year, according to the CDC. Healthcare costs account for only 11 percent of that. The primary cost is lost job productivity.

Drug Abuse: The aggregate cost from drug abuse in the USA is $1 trillion, including costs for medical care and criminal justice. Janet Yellen, former chair of the Federal Reserve, attributes drug abuse to a lack of job opportunities among prime-age workers. Other factors include escape from pain, as with opioid addiction.

Gun Violence: Gun violence costs an average of $700 per year, per person, with an annual hit to the economy of $229 billion, reports Mother Jones. Direct expenses for emergency and medical care from gun violence are $8.6 billion. "It does not matter whether we believe that guns kill people or that people kill people with guns," wrote a team of doctors in the April 2017 Annals of Internal Medicine. "The result is the same: A public health crisis."

The Obesity Crisis

America, the "land of plenty," has ample portion sizes feeding our waistlines. The National Heart, Lung, and Blood Institute calculated that in the past 20 years, a simple bagel grew three inches in diameter to six inches. A cheeseburger grew from 3.5 to 8 ounces. A "normal" serving of sugar-laden soda grew from 6.5 to 20 ounces.

The CDC reports almost 40 percent of all U.S. adults are obese as are nearly 20 percent of all adolescents. NBC News in 2017 said the "obesity crisis" appears more unstoppable than ever.

Obesity is the underlying cause, a contributor or a complicator of heart disease, stroke, high blood pressure, diabetes, gout, gallbladder disease and gallstones, osteoarthritis, and breathing issues like sleep apnea and asthma. Being overweight or obese further is associated with increased risk for 13 types of cancer, accounting for 40 percent of all the cancers diagnosed in the United States.

Other countries use taxes to fight obesity. Mexico's sugar tax cut soda consumption by 5.5 percent the first year and 9.7 percent the next. Similar taxes are working in Canada, United Kingdom, Ireland, Portugal, France, Saudi Arabia, South Africa, Australia, and Thailand. Portugal added a salt tax on fattening snacks.

Seven countries have started food fights with junk food. Mexico, Chile, Norway France, India, Japan, and Australia seek to motivate behavioral change in the population. These efforts range from taxing the fat content in prepared foods to banning advertising to children that use toys as incentives to buy sugary foods. Each approaches the obesity problem differently, yet each aims to shift unhealthy behavior by raising the costs at decision time for unhealthy behaviors.

All these countries have national health coverage, so they can use governmental taxing authority to impact behaviors that increase the cost to health care programs. America could learn from them.

In the USA, where two-thirds of all Americans are obese, no such national efforts exist. We have local initiatives. Philadelphia introduced a tax on sugary drinks that cut soda consumption 38 percent in 30 days and 40 percent in 60 days, reported Philadelphia Magazine, and energy drink consumption fell 64 percent. Consumption of bottled water rose 58 percent.

The New York Board of Health tried to tax sugary drinks, but an

> **Countries with national health coverage use governmental authority to impact health behaviors.**

appeals court found the city exceeded its authority, Beverage Daily reported. I believe a win for sugary drinks was a loss for health.

Embracing the digital life (TV, games, internet) contributes to a sedentary lifestyle, which contributes to obesity. The State of Obesity estimates 45 percent of all U.S. adults are not active enough to get daily health benefits. Diseases related to inactivity cause $117 billion in direct healthcare costs. Our vaunted healthcare system does little to address this source for high healthcare demand and rising costs. At best, health insurance reimburses a gym membership.

Employers are showing leadership by matching economics with behavior. Some levy higher payroll health insurance deductions for employees that smokes or test with a high Body Mass Index (BMI), a ratio of body fat to height and weight. Some offer employee benefits for gym memberships (and usage). Others design offices for more walking around with more stairs to climb. It's a good start.

Genetics and Health

Genetics are powerful when it comes to our health and longevity. Genetics impact 30 percent of our premature deaths. We benefit by knowing in advance our genetic predispositions to diabetes or kidney disease or obesity. We might act to avert illnesses. Early interventions like a change of diet or monitoring can make a huge difference in not only our own lives but in reducing overall medical care costs.

Genetic testing plays a role in identifying fetuses likely to be born with life-ending or threatening birth defects. Sampling amniotic fluid during pregnancy, amniocentesis, a screening for fetal abnormalities, is nearly routine. Such testing can detect the likelihood of sickle cell disease, Down syndrome, cystic fibrosis, muscular dystrophy, Tay-Sachs disease, or any diseases where the brain and spinal column do not develop properly, such as spina bifida and anencephaly.

How do we act on that information?

In Iceland, infant Down Syndrome has been virtually eliminated by fetal testing and abortions, reported CBS News "On Assignment." In developed nations, termination of pregnancies for birth defects is becoming widespread, even in countries with strong anti-abortion cultures and laws and customs.

The Genetic Literacy Project reports genetic testing is becoming part of matchmaking for arranged marriages among Hasidic Jews, who do not sanction abortion. Hasidic high school students get their blood drawn for genetic testing. Later, when a match is proposed, the matchmaker or families use the tests to spot a risk of genetic diseases or birth defects, then they bless or discourage the marriage.

Environmental Factors

Twenty percent of us are at risk of premature death from social factors and environmental factors.

Among lower-income groups, a link exists between lower health status and higher health costs. Lack of education limits employment, limiting income, which limits access to quality food, limits access to healthy working and living conditions, limits access to quality child care, limits access to health care services, increasing health care costs, which increases medical debt, which is a pox upon society.

Nothing in the scope of health insurance can or will address the ecological and social factors contributing to higher health care costs. The healthcare system is not demanding upstream solutions.

Today's anti-regulation wave erodes environmental protections, yet the impact on healthcare costs should be considered.

More than 1,000 people a day are admitted to hospitals because of chronic lung diseases like asthma, costing the nation $56 billion annually in both direct costs (such as hospitalization) and indirect costs (such as missed work and decreased productivity), according to the National Environmental Education Foundation.

Air pollution contributes to 16,000 premature births each year, adding $760 million in direct healthcare costs plus $3.57 billion in lost productivity costs from physical and mental disabilities, reports Business Insider. The Rand Corporation found that between 2005 and 2007 in California, air pollution added $193 million in hospital costs — Medicare paid $104 million, Medicaid paid $28 million, and private insurances paid the balance of $56 million.

Theory and Reality

Cigna CEO David Cordani told Business Insider magazine, "We spend the majority of our money and resources addressing people once they're sick. We need to spend more of our resources keeping people healthy in the first case, and identifying people who are at risk of health events, and lowering those health risks."

No amount of tinkering with insurance models will change the fact health care costs reflect the demand for care and the costs to deliver care. The demand side and the structural side of care delivery add to the costs of delivering care services. The health care industry inadvertently has been allowed to become a voracious monster that threatens to devour every dollar of America's GDP.

> **The healthcare system is not demanding upstream solutions.**

Hospitals have emerged as the concentrated economic powers in our healthcare system. They have evolved from the local community institutions into networks of care providers composed of urgent care centers (once denigrated as a "doc-in-the-box"), ambulatory surgery centers (ACS), and hospital-owned practices employing 42 percent of all practicing physicians, says Becker's Hospital Review.

In theory, such a system could provide great benefits for patients. In-system treatment ought to assure coordination among caregivers, who share patient medical records to avoid costly duplicative testing and conflicting drug interactions. In theory, all this lowers the cost of health care by squeezing out unnecessary services within the delivery of care. Such a health care structure should lower costs and improve quality. What could be better?

Reality is different. These systems have become additive to health care costs rather than reductive. Hospital-dominated systems put the economic needs of the system before the fiscal impact on patients. Revenue is produced by the system and for the system (a pay-into system). Efficiencies and economies benefit the system. Patients pay more in the process, as do their health insurance companies.

Market Watch tells a tale that is far too common. Jackie Thennes switched to an in-network doctor at a health system facility near her. Her bill suddenly included charges for each doctor visit along with something extra — an added $235 "facility fee."

Concern for maximizing mission has been replaced by concern for maximizing margins.

National Healthcare Policy

All this brings us back to the central problem of medical debt, the proposals and solutions and schemes for who pays and how.

Regardless of your support for national health insurance, or your opposition, the reality is that the crisis in health insurance coverage and affordability is a crisis in the cost of delivering healthcare.

Hiding care delivery costs in the current insurance model, or in a nationalized healthcare tax scheme, does not change the structure of care delivery. Neither approach resolves all the factors driving the demand for care. Even if a national health insurance program were created, the issue of costs would continue to be a problem.

Opposition to national health insurance, in part, is from a belief the costs will be too great. Given the current trajectory of spending, this objection is valid — up to a point. The Centers for Medicare and Medicaid Services (CMS) projected annual healthcare spending by 2026 will surpass $5.7 trillion dollars. Investor's Business Daily estimates that a "Medicare for All" plan would add $32 trillion to federal spending over 10 years, which is $3.2 trillion a year. The current system or a single-payer system will both be expensive.

> The current system or a single-payer system will both be expensive.

Health insurance is only a scheme to finance health care services. Whether premiums are funded by individual purchase, by employers paying for care benefits or by taxes, it's just a mechanism for funding the healthcare system to provide care services. Vested interests want to keep the current system in place.

Focusing only on health insurance misses the real issues — the demand for services and the costly ways that services are delivered. Both factors must be addressed.

For instance, a nation concerned about the quality of its citizens' lives can use taxes to motivate healthier behaviors that reduce a need for care services. Tax deductions for charity donations motivate the generosity of taxpayers. Home mortgage deductions motivate home ownership for family and community stability. By increasing taxes on unhealthy behaviors, the cost of such behaviors shifts to the point of personal decision. It's wrong to make the cost of care a barrier to treating the consequences of unhealthy behaviors. If costs delay care, it results in still higher costs and poorer outcomes. This is tragic if an illness stems from factors outside a person's control, such as genetic ailments or respiratory disease caused by secondhand smoke.

The healthcare industry cannot be expected to reform itself, to become efficient and effective, to find ways of delivering care faster, better and cheaper. It is not structured to do so. Hospitals' focus on profits do not reduce their costs to the communities they serve. From noble charities, they've evolved into economic carnivores.

Separate silos for health care delivery and public health or social services just is not working. Underfunding public health and social services results in a greater demand for costlier healthcare services. Likewise, underregulating environmental quality issues results in a greater demand for all healthcare services. Our healthcare silos raise our costs. We need a holistic approach to healthcare costs.

> We need a holistic approach to healthcare costs.

The totality of costs being spent on medical care, public health and social services needs to be considered along with what we know reduces the need for care. Let's allocate services accordingly. A national healthcare policy needs to be established as a guide.

What matters most is caring for the ill and injured. Returning to this focus will produce a healthier population, which will reduce the cost of care, and so reduce or eliminate medical debt.

A national healthcare policy needs to support a country that is healthy and an economy that is strong. From such a policy, decisions can be made to support the goal of health, not just care delivery.

Tax policy influencing self-care decisions need not result in some "nanny state" that erodes personal responsibility. The actual costs of pollution, in terms of health and productivity, for instance, need to be moved from the healthcare system to the polluters. For me, that would be taking responsibility for our economic freedoms. We treat corporations as persons under the law, so accept responsibility.

From a national healthcare policy aimed at improving the health of Americans can flow sensible health benefit plans that promote and support preventative and routine care as well as early interventions for illness along with health maintenance for chronic care.

The structure for delivering care needs to be reconstituted for the betterment of the full population. A sustainable, affordable funding model then becomes a possibility, be it insurance, Medicare for All, or some other national health plan.

The present system is rigged against citizen health. This is being done not by design, not by a cabal of evil doers, but by the historical evolution of our healthcare delivery structure. We need an evolution to higher thinking for the health of everyone in America.

To paraphrase the famous old Pogo comic strip, "We have met the problem, and it is us."

*My doctor gave me six months to live,
but when I couldn't pay the bill
he gave me six months more.*

— Walter Matthau

CHAPTER 10

Personal and General Medical Debt Solutions

Craig Antico

Every day I see our healthcare system causing financial ruin to millions of Americans, their friends and families. Many of them would be financially ruined no matter what they or we can do. That's unacceptable. I want to help ensure this does not happen to them or you. I later will speak to systemic things we can do as a country to avoid those outcomes.

Until then, let's get personal.

Illnesses or accidents often cause unexpected shocks, and material hardship often ensues. There are useful steps you can take — or your friends and family can take — that are in your personal control, so you can mitigate the risk of the medical debt hardship.

Nothing is sadder to me than seeing people make poor decisions about their own health care and wellness because of ignorance or an unwillingness to act. Nothing makes me angrier than the number of people in positions of authority who are unwilling to educate and support people in need, so they can actually help themselves.

There is no other nation in the world like the United States that tries as hard to make up for the system disparities, inequalities and government inefficiencies, or that donates more time and money for the good of others. When we Americans are made aware of others' unmet needs, such as after a wildfire or hurricane, we do our best as givers, and as recipients of giving. This gives me hope.

Personal Responsibility Solutions

Many of us are just one illness or accident away from financial ruin or material hardship from medical debt. Hardship can occur for you and others when you or another person...

1. Doesn't take or have the time to stay current on their bills.
2. Waits until they're in a crisis to act.
3. Doesn't read through the medical bills they get.
4. Asks you or another to pay any bill for them.
5. Ignores health care billing notices.
6. Puts bills on a credit card (worse if you co-signed).
7. Doesn't feel the need to have any health insurance.
8. Doesn't understand that if you secured insurance for them, then you are doomed to pay for their medical debt hardship.

When it comes to material hardship, I've seen it all in my work. As one whose family has experienced material hardship, I wish to help you avoid or mitigate such deep scars by teaching you how to take much better personal responsibility for your own health care costs.

If you have everything under full control, and you're properly insured, you can ignore the tips below. These

> **Take better personal responsibility for your own health care costs.**

are tips I've garnered in the 30 years that I've been in this business of cleaning up the debt mess created by our healthcare system. I've also learned what to do from my own hardship. These can help.

Below is a self-help guide with basic how-to information.

Learn About Health Insurance

Research how health insurance works and doesn't work (reread this book). Understand the concepts of co-insurance, co-payments, deductibles, and those out-of-network benefits and pitfalls.

If you are insured, approximately 25-30 percent of your cost for healthcare comes out of your pocket in the form of deductibles, co-pays and co-insurance. Know exactly what your own plan covers. Read the fine print. According to The Commonwealth Fund, being uninsured or underinsured affects 68 million people in America.

Determine What Services Are Covered In-Network

If you live in a region with only one hospital, you are especially vulnerable to not having any in-network doctors. However, this can happen in any hospital if they participate in few insurance plans.

Before you need care, find out if which local care providers are covered by your in-network insurance plan, such as radiologists, anesthesiologists and laboratories. The hospital may be in-network, but every caregiver in the hospital might not be.

Above all, find out in advance of a medical crisis whether or not your local ambulance company and hospital emergency room staff is in-network. They may not be. If not, you could get a bill five to ten times the cost of in-network charges for the same services.

Know Consumer Rights Around 'Balance Billing'

A New England Journal of Medicine study in 2016 found that 22 percent of emergency room visits nationally involve care by an out-of-network doctor, putting the patient at risk of a surprise medical bill, known as "balance billing," or billing for the unpaid balance. Balance billing is prohibited for people on Medicaid or Medicare.

Zack Cooper, assistant professor of health policy and economics at Yale University, stated in an interview with Kellie Schmitt of the USC Annenberg Center for Health Journalism, "These sorts of surprise bills can tally up into the hundreds or thousands of dollars and really wreak financial havoc on people's lives."

Lindy Washburn at NorthJersey covered the governor of New Jersey, Phil Murphy, in April 2018 signing a new law against balance billing, calling it "one of the strongest consumer protection laws in the country." Murphy said at the signing that an estimated 168,000 patients get "out-of-network bills that total $420 million annually," which adds $1 billion annually to health costs.

Other states have similar bills proposed or enacted. No national law exists. So, always ask if your care provider is in-network.

Examine Bills Carefully

Adria Goldman Gross from MedWise Insurance Advocacy in Monroe, New York, warns that "about eighty percent of all medical bills have errors." You need to know what to look for. Gross says to search the internet to find the "reasonable and customary charges" for the medical procedure codes on your bill (and what they mean). Compare what you find to your own charges.

Mistakes on bills often are due to miscoding, but wait 30-45 days before calling because it often takes three months for insurance billing to go through. If you are on Medicare, carefully review your quarterly Medicare Summary Notice.

Get everything pinned down in advance, she says, stressing the importance of written estimates: "Whatever agreed fee amount you have with your medical provider, make sure you have it in writing."

Beware of Facility Fees

Hospital-owned physician practices charge "facilities fees" above the usual service charge. In Washington state, for instance, a patient paid $125 out-of-pocket to visit an employed doctor, but visit costs skyrocketed to more than $500 to reflect a new facility fee charge.

The Physician Advocacy Institute asserts facility fees are being charged much more than before because hospitals now own about 30 percent of physician practices and employ over 42 percent of all physicians (a 100 percent increase since 2012).

These practices have the legal right to charge facilities fees, even if a physician practice is off-campus from the hospital. The problem is that patient don't expect to get charged more when they are going to the same place they always went for care services. Facility fees can occur even if the doctor is just "affiliated" with a hospital.

> Alway ask in advance of the visit if you will be charged a facility fee

Ask in advance of a visit if you will be charged a facility fee. If so, find out whether your procedure can be done at another location that doesn't charge a fee. Always ask *before* the service is rendered because fighting the fee afterwards is close to impossible.

Always File Out-of-Network Claims

An insurance company can process and pay an out-of-network bill as much as seven years after an "OON" bill has been generated. This can happen even after a bill was paid by you, by friends or by family ($55 billion each year is given by friends and family for medical expenses and debt repayment). So, always submit your out-of-network charges to your insurance company.

If you are not filing a claim for your own benefit, do it to repay the friends and family who gave to you until it hurt.

Do not ask your doctor for hospital file the OON claim for you, It's not in their interest to make sure you get reimbursed. Either do it yourself or go to GetBetter.co to have them process your claim.

With more than $115 billion a year being billed OON, and an accumulated $450-500 billion left unpaid over the last seven years, there's a potential of recovering about $45-60 million dollars from insurance companies. Get OON it!

Determine if Underinsured. If Uninsured, Get Insurance

The cheapest health insurance likely is no bargain. If you make less than two times the Federal Poverty Level (FPL), your deductible should not exceed five percent of your gross income. If you earn more, your deductible should not exceed 10 percent of your gross income. If you earn $30,000, your deductible should be not more than $1,500 a year. If you earn $60,000, is $6,000 a year.

If you do not yet have insurance, or your deductible is higher than the above guidelines, your family is underinsured. If you have one major illness or accident, you and your family are vulnerable to material hardship that could last from three to five years.

Determine Eligibility for Charity Care Before You Need It.

Search the internet for your local hospital name and the phrase, "financial assistance." Find the hospital "financial assistance policy," perhaps called a "charity care policy." Independent doctors do not offer charity care, as a rule, for they cannot afford to do so.

Most hospitals offer free charity care for low income patients. To qualify, you usually need to make below two times (200 percent) the FPL. If you are over that, there will usually be a sliding scale from 10 percent to 80 percent of the bill you will end up paying, if approved — but you must ask. (While online, find a Federal Poverty Level guidelines calculator to assess your situation.)

FYI: We as a nation every year on average give to charity about two percent of our gross domestic product (GDP). What's stunning is that the 33 percent of the population that earns less than two times the FPL — about $40,000-$50,000 — are the most generous givers to charity as well as to needy friends and family (F&F). As a percentage of adjusted gross income, this segment gives away more than those in much higher income brackets. Lower-income people give more, even if it brings them hardship, because they know first-hand what a big difference generosity makes in people's lives.

Apply for Medicaid in Case of Low Income

Although low income lasts a lifetime for some, poverty is often a temporary situation. I'm talking from experience. Medicaid is the health insurance for all low-income citizens who cannot afford their medical care expenses. Income qualification criteria vary by state, so contact your state Medicaid office to see if you qualify. Your child may be eligible for Medicaid even if you are not.

If you qualify, Medicaid may fully pay for the medical expenses already incurred, but only within a certain timeframe, about 90-180 days. Apply as soon as possible after receiving a medical bill.

If you are up to age 26 and on your parent's insurance, consider applying for Medicaid. We don't know anybody on Medicaid with medical debt problems, including recent graduates looking for a job. Consider yourself fortunate if you

> **Medicaid may fully pay for medical expenses already incurred.**

have parental plan coverage, yet they'll consider themselves fortunate if you have a major illness or accident and your Medicaid spares them from financial ruin.

Communicate with Providers and Collectors if in Hardship

Do not be one of the 30 percent of all the people with hospital accounts at collection agencies who earlier had qualified for charity care but did not accept it, or did not know to ask for it.

If you did not apply for charity care, and if paying the bill you received will cause you and your family real hardship, contact your hospital or their collector, or answer their call.

Only Visit the ER in a Genuine Emergency

Call your doctor if an issue is not life-threatening. Go to the ER if your doctor says to go. My spouse did make that call, but she was in excruciating pain and later couldn't remember who said to go to the ER. We had to pay a $700 ER bill that could have been a $150 co-pay. So, get the name of whom talks to you at the doctor's office, note the time you spoke, and have them make a notation in your records that they felt your condition warranted an emergency visit.

Pay only Three to Six Percent of Your Gross Income on Out-of-Pocket Expenses or Past Medical Debt

Financial hardship can occur when medical expenses reach as little as two percent of gross income. Only you know how much you can afford to pay for out-of-pocket (OOP) medical expenses and past debt. Your savings, a second job, or family and friends can all mitigate hardship, foster resiliency and reduce stress.

Although research shows that most people experience hardship when their OOP expenses rise above 2.5 percent of gross income, you may have more or less resiliency than others.

Stay within three to six percent of your gross income. Make a yearly projection of up to six percent of your gross income. Only pay out what you can afford. Even if you are getting collection calls, be resolute that you will not stop taking your medications, going to the doctor, paying rent or utilities, or putting tires on your car. No one can force you to pay for a bill instead of life necessities. You always control who and how much you pay.

> No debt collector can force you to pay for a bill instead of necessities.

Don't Pay with Credit Cards or Interest-Bearing Loans

The main way medical debt from a hospital or doctor becomes an interest-bearing "debt" is when you ignore it, get sued, ignore that or lose the case, and find a judgment entered against you.

Trouble can ensue if you pay the bill with a credit card or loan. If you have debt at a high-interest rate debt, such as a credit card or a payday loan, get to know the "Rule of 76." (Low rate loans like home equity lines use the "Rule of 72.") Researching both rules will help you understand the likely cost of using financial instruments to pay off medical expenses or medical debt.

The Rule of 76 calculates how soon the amount you owe will double. To do it, divide your interest rate (say 24 percent) into 76 (76 ÷ 24 = 3.17). This is the number of years it will take to double how much you owe. The Rule of 76 tells you that the $3,000 you put on a credit card turns into $6,000 in about three years! Ouch.

If possible, make an interest-free installment payment agreement with the medical provider. No credit is needed for that, and it won't show on your credit report. Never miss that payment!

Start or Max-Out Your Health Savings Account

A 2017 Kaiser Family Foundation survey found 46 percent of enrollees in high-deductible health plans (HDHP) report difficulty affording deductibles. About 60 percent of those with employer-sponsored health insurance have high deductible of at least $1,300 for an individual and $2,750 for a family. A Health Savings Account (HSA) can foster resiliency and avert medically-induced hardship. Try to fund the maximum annual contribution in your HSA.

An HSA has a significant tax benefit. You don't pay taxes on the money put into the plan, nor do you pay taxes on the amount you use on medical expenses or premiums. Once you are on Medicare, you can't contribute to an HSA, so start now. Stop funding an HSA six months before you join Medicare to avoid HSA issues.

IRS rules for 2018 let you contribute up to $3,450 per year as an individual ,or $6,900 if you have family coverage. The IRS allows a catch-up contribution up to $1,000 a year for those age 55 or over.

Sign up for Medicare on Time to Avoid Penalties

The Forbes Finance Council warns about significant penalties for late enrollment into Medicare. These penalties accumulate the longer you wait to enroll and can be very costly. You can avoid any penalties by signing up for Medicare when you are first eligible.

> If you can afford a good Medicare supplemental plan, be sure to buy one.

You have a seven-month initial enrollment period starting three months before and after you turn 65. Enroll in Medicare Parts A, B and D during this period if you don't have better health insurance coverage.

Medicare only covers 80 percent of an authorized charge. If you can afford a good Medicare supplemental plan, be sure to buy one. That 20 percent difference can mean the difference between solvency and hardship in case you have a major illness or injury.

Prepare for Healthcare Expenses in Retirement

A 65-year-old couple that retires today would need an estimated $280,000 to cover their expected health care costs in retirement, according to a Fidelity analysis. Acquiring supplemental coverage is one of the most important things you can do to limit or completely avoid medical debt during retirement.

Get The Caregiving Tax Credit

With more than 25 million seniors living below 250 percent of the FPL, more caregivers are needed, and families just can't cope. If you are one of the 35 million adult children caring for a parent, or one of the 15 million caring for a spouse, or one of the 35 million parents taking care of adult children with disabilities, you are keenly aware of the costs involved. The average paid for OOP expenses per year is more than $,7000, but figure in lost wages, less Social Security benefits later in life, added stress, and other hidden costs.

Those providing care for a family member can get a tax credit under the Credit for Caring Act. According to AARP, the IRS gives eligible family caregivers the opportunity to receive a tax credit for 30 percent of qualified expenses above $2,000 paid to help a loved one. The maximum credit amount is $3,000.

Get Compensated as a Caregiver

There also are programs and mechanisms that enable you, as the caregiver for a family member, that can ease the added expense and lost income — paying you for your service. These payers could be a long-term care insurance plan, Medicaid or worker's compensation claim. The VA may honor a claim if the care receiver is a veteran.

The National Academy of Elder Law Attorneys is the leading attorney network working with consumers on the legal problems of aging Americans as well as people of all ages with disabilities. They can help you draft a formal "eldercare contract," normally between family members, which outlines care responsibilities and provides a way for a caregiver to be paid. Such an agreement potentially clears up any confusion among family members.

A care agreement lets the family pool resources to pay for a caregiver, if the care recipient lacks means. If the care recipient has ample resources, an agreement can mitigates feuds between family members on who inherits money or gifts. It further can ensure the caregiver is treated with respect, especially if a caregiver must stop working to help a loved one.

If your loved one is a veteran, contact Veteran Directed Home and Community-Based Services (VDHCBS), which pays vet family members to act as caregivers.

> **A care agreement lets a family pool resources to pay for a caregiver.**

Use a Medicaid-Paid Caregiving Program

Medicaid in your state may offer a way to get paid for taking care of a family member, friend or neighbor. New York State offers the Consumer Directed Personal Assistance Program (CD-PAP), a Medicaid-funded program that allows care recipients to hire almost any caregiver they choose, including the family member currently providing care. Freedom Care NY provides services statewide.

Most state Medicaid programs offer some form of self-directed care, which is used by more than 800,000 patients nationwide, according to an Open Minds report authored by Athena Mandros, a market intelligence editor focusing on Medicaid trends.

The above tips are by no means comprehensive, but if you apply them, you may spare yourself from hardship due to medical debt.

General Solutions

The cost of health care is expected to double in the next seven to ten years with income at a slower growth rate. It doesn't matter who pays each medical bill — government already pays 70 percent of the costs — it will be impossible to pay for all care without a revolution in cost reduction or an increase in effectiveness and wellness.

While we search for a way to increase wellness, which will reduce the health care costs trajectory, we can make a significant impact through the following strategies:

- Shifts in data sharing, trusts, ownership, control, monitoring.
- More transparent, responsive, impactful financial assistance policy education, plan design and real-time delivery.
- More finance industry social responsibility.
- Use of shared burden platforms for elimination of medically-induced financial hardship.

Make Charity Care and Medicaid Opt-Out

A simple solution for part of our medical debt epidemic, at least on the nonprofit hospital side (where more than a third of medical debt is created), would be to make charity care and Medicaid opt-out. Those who qualify under the financial assistance policy (FAP) of the hospital would automatically get vital care for free. Patients could decline or opt-out of free care, but few would, I expect.

Hospitals until now have required patients to provide extensive verification of income, assets or hardship to qualify for charity care. The onus has been on the patients so too few even apply.

RIP can now provide hospitals (using their current technology), with our data and analytics to connect their clinical data with federal Health and Human Services networks for patient verifications. This innovative linkage between a Health Information Exchange (HIE) and Community Information Exchange (CIE) shows great promise for identifying qualified and verified charity care patients along with providing medical debt abolishment on the spot.

As a proof-of concept, RIP is engaged in a first-of-its-kind pilot with 2-1-1 San Diego, a social service resource and information hub. Using their CIE, we are connecting two participating hospitals and 6,000 health and human services providers in San Diego to identify charity care cases, and to abolish medical debt for qualified patients. (Jerry gave a detailed description of the project earlier as an example of the John Oliver Effect.) The project suggests the possibilities.

Build 'Data Trusts' Where Consumers Control Their Own Data

Wellness and health care services, like all ventures, spend a lot of money for personal data to identify who needs their services, then the spend to improve their services to make them more attractive.

Personal data on our wellness (mental, physical, and emotional), our finances and consumer behavior, is and should be private. Lack of privacy breeds distrust between consumers and providers.

Products or services can be designed and marketed more ethically if we'll create a trustworthy medical data system controlled by people themselves. Health care services could be provided to people in real time, based on reliable anonymized data about people, families, and communities — driven by evidence of data-informed impacts. This could lower health care costs across the board in all sectors.

To accomplish this worthy goal, I support using the data flow science created and pioneered over two decades by OBASHI in Scotland, which is accredited and deployed internationally.

I envision "data trusts" where people (patients and consumers) could own, control and monitor their private personal data, which would legally belong to them, not to corporations or the state.

> 'Data trusts' would let us own, control and monitor our private personal data.

Europe is way ahead of America in adopting this principle of personal data ownership. I propose we unite the patient protections of the Health Insurance Portability and Accountability Act (HIPAA) with the privacy protections of secure data trusts.

Have Specialty Finance Companies Abolish Medical Debt

Hospitals and doctors have started getting out of the business of letting you owe them — incur medical debt. They want an immediate payment. They elect not to participate in any insurance plans at all, government or private. Thery take only cash, or have you provide a credit card. Some bring in a bank specialty finance company, such as CareCredit. You may owe a bank without ever realizing that you don't owe anything directly to the hospital or doctor.

In my mind, this trend could be harmful to patients financially, as I discussed in an earlier chapter. To offset the risks of medical debt owed to banks rather than to care providers, I propose that these specialty finance companies establish a fund to abolish (forgive) the medical debt of those in hardship. Such a fund could be created by each company or the special finance industry acting in unison.

Build a Charity Fund to Pay Caregivers for Caregiving

Caaring caregivers are burdened medical debt fro mgiving care. Caregiving is now more and more of a hardship for our dwindling caregiver base. We need create a safety net for them. We need more education on all the programs out there for caregivers. Caregiving itself needs to be better funded. I propose that we unite to establish state and national charitable funds for this purpose.

About $400 billion in caregiving services are rendered each year, and much of that is lost income. This is the same amount, remember, as the $400 billion that citizens, corporations and foundations give to charities every year. Caregivers rarely get trained in the financial matters affecting them. Few even know that some states and entities actual pay F&F caregivers. We can do more to support them.

Abolish the Debt-of-Necessity Causing Material Hardship

RIP, with a $500,000 donation from a caring couple, abolished $50 million in veterans' medical debt in late 2018 as part of a larger donation that wiped out more than $250 million in medical debt. We forgave debt for those in hardship afterthey incurred medical debt-of-necessity from unexpected illnesses or injures. We helped, certainly, but what else can be done? A lot more debt is out there.

Shift Who Pays for Severely Past Due, Unpayable Debt

I've run collection companies all my adult life, and more than 50 percent of the collection work done by my industry is for medical debt. Before founding RIP with Jerry Ashton, also a debt collections veteran, we worked in a broad industry that made $19 billion a year in revenue — $8 billion from medical debt collections, $6 billion in debt settlement and debt consolidation, and $5 billion in repairing people's credit. The industry earned an additional $50 billion from debts settlements collected for creditor clients.

I estimate that 20-25 percent of those debtors were in hardship at the time they paid those debts. If we educated those in hardship to safely and privately self-identify their hardship, our communities could pay off their debts for them through chairitable debt buys and abolishments. If we'd help share the debt burdens, we'd reduce material hardship to practically nothing.

> A small shift in our national wealth can make a large dent in U.S. medical debt.

A shift of just $2 billion in our national wealth to boy older medical debt (at a penny on the dollar) could abolish $200 billion in medical debt, eradicating virtually all medical debt hardship in the country. Such wide debt forgiveness is very possible with enough donations for debt forgiveness by those without debt and by those with debt but who can donate without hardship.

Given $1 trillion in unpayable healthcare bills in America, such a small shift in our national wealth can make a large dent in U.S. medical debt. If we reduce this pressure form our economy, we may then find more permanent answers for finally ending medical debt, such as increasing wellness, reducing costs, and changing how we finance health care in our nation.

A hospital bed is a parked taxi with the meter running.

— Groucho Marx

CHAPTER 11

National Health Care: To Be or Not To Be?

Jerry Ashton

We're in a particularly difficult period of time in society today (or what passes for society). When it comes to healthcare, forget about "reasoned discourse." You are damned if you pick a side, such as for or against single-payer, damned for the side you pick, or condemned by all sides for not picking any side.

As we three authors have made clear in our own ways, blaming others avoids responsibility. A clearly destructive path is being taken, but we have consented to it. Fixed positions on healthcare are now required for every social group, economic class, religion, or political persuasion. A justification for any position will and must be found. Minds are closed. Why argue? Move on. Nothing to see here.

Meanwhile, our broken healthcare system screams for change. We are experiencing a "global warming" in healthcare economics. Every tiny degree that costs go up for insurance, drugs, hospitals and other care, in turn, creates a hotter, costlier future. Deniers refuse to admit that our structure ensures costs and medical debt will rise.

Our society is as fractured as our healthcare system. Each given healthcare "solution" is well defended, and too often by those same interests that are creating the problem. Some of us feel locked into the current system by a career or paycheck. Others of us are devoted to a bedrock ideology of right and wrong. Our refusal to compromise is moral, and all doubts are treason.

What stance are we willing to give up to make healthcare work? What are we willing to do to make America healthier, equitable and sustainable? No matter what solution we pick, implementation will not be easy, and that solution may never be perfect.

Is medical debt forgiveness the solution? Well, yes and no.

The "no" is because medical debt forgiveness treats the symptom but does not cure the disease. The many sources of medical debt reside "upstream." Righting a wrong by forgiving debt, however sincere and well-intended, is not a real solution for ridding America of medical debt. Given $1 trillion of medical debt in America, and rising, even if RIP can grow to abolish two or three billion dollars in medical debt every year, that will not change the existing healthcare system. Debt forgiveness, by itself, will never make a real dent in all the debt that has been created, is being created and is yet to be created. We need a structural change in the system.

> Medical debt forgiveness treats the symptom but does not cure the disease.

The "yes" is because RIP is becoming a voice that calls attention to the problem of medical debt and the process of finding solutions that work. As a 501(c)(3) tax-exempt charitable organization under U.S law, we cannot directly engage in politics. However, we can ally ourselves with people and organizations active in the monumental efforts to inform America and change public opinion. We can help to repair our nation's conscience as well as its wallet.

Our charity will keep fulfilling our mandate of debt forgiveness, making a persistent person-by-person, family-by-family dent in the financial anguish and pain of the medical debt burdening millions of people. We are grateful to be their champions.

We further will call public attention to the problem of medical debt and the healthcare system creating it. We will raise awareness, touch hearts, educate with integrity, and call for action. By our sheer numbers, the collective voice and actions of those concerned about the issue will finally end medical debt.

Within RIP, we would love to see our charity put out of business. No medical debt would mean no need to forgive it. This is likely a ways off, but it can happen once Americans agree we need essential changes in the financial model of healthcare delivery.

The tide is turning. I see Americans removing their blinders and challenging the status quo, honestly looking at alternatives. We are seeing that not only are we our brother's keeper, we are our brother. This final chapter looks at ways to create such positive changes.

A Modern Barn Raising

Back in the 19th and 20th century, if a rural family's livelihood was ruined by a major financial loss, like a barn destroyed by a fire or tornado, the community would show up and pitch in, unpaid, to build a replacement barn. Some contributed labor, some lumber or nails, others money, but they all contributed from their hearts.

There was enlightened self-interest in those community actions. People recognized, "It could be me someday," so they all pitched in vigorously, even joyfully (as with Habitat for Humanity). People knew that should a disaster happen in their own lives, their friends, neighbors, and relatives would return the social investment.

Today, for the donors and fans of RIP Medical Debt, perhaps at an unconscious level, we serve a similar role for social investment. Many of our donors know, at some level, that medical debt on their credit report, bankruptcy, job loss, failure to finance a car or rent an apartment, or other issues, could well be in their future. We accept that our own "barn" could need raising someday.

> If nothing changes in healthcare financing, none of us are safe from catastrophic medical bills.

If nothing changes in healthcare financing, none of us are safe from catastrophic medical bills. Your own family will not save you. Social rank will not save you. Wealth will not save you. Education will not save you.

The failure of the current system is epitomized in an October 3, 2018, obituary for the Nobel Prize-winning physicist, Leon Lederman, age 96. His wife told the Associated Press that in 2015 he'd sold his Nobel Prize at auction for $765,000 "to help pay for medical bills and care."

Therefore, in the spirit of civic education and open discourse, let's take a look at the four most common solutions proposed for improving healthcare and lowering medical costs:

1. Repeal and Replace Obamacare.
2. Regulate insurance and drug prices.
3. Add a Medicare option to the ACA.
4. Offer Medicare for All or single-payer healthcare

A caveat: None of what follows is comprehensive. You will not find here all you need to know. Our goal is raising public awareness. What you do with that awareness — such as seeking more education or becoming more actively involved — is up to you.

Repeal and Replace Obamacare

The battle cry of "Repeal and Replace" grew silent in response to voter outrage in the 2018 mid-term elections, rejecting politicians who favored stopping coverage for preexisting conditions. Still, the case is instructive should this idea ever be resurrected.

Writer and gadfly John Hecht wrote a great 2017 Bustle article, "Repeal and Replace is Dead: A Definitive Timeline of Republicans' Zombie Obamacare Bill That No One Can Kill." Hecht tracked the Republican efforts and gave reasons for its failure.

The chief reason was that "Republican lawmakers couldn't quite stomach it." Defunding the ACA would drive up health insurance premiums to stratospheric levels. Repealing the ACA subsidy would cause 32 million voters to lose their insurance. Also chilling House GOP enthusiasm was the pummeling at town hall meetings by angry constituents, who in 2018 voted many of them out of office.

A number of cobbled-together iterations failed to get the votes. A bold thumbs down by Sen. John McCain hammered the stake through the heart of his party's one possibly viable offering.

When the GOP "skinny bill" failed to pass, Sen. Lindsey Graham summed up the GOP's seven years of trying to repeal and replace the ACA. (Replace with what?) He said, "I thought everybody else knew what the hell they were talking about, but apparently not."

Undeterred, the GOP Congress and the Supreme Court undercut the individual mandate, giving a basis for Republican state attorneys general to file a lawsuit against the ACA. The Trump administration did not defend the hated "Obamacare." A federal district court judge in Texas, ignoring the principle of severability, ruled in December 2018 that the entire ACA is unconstitutional.

A group of states governed by Democrats appealed the ruling to a higher circuit court. The case could end up in the Supreme Court. Meanwhile, the ACA remains in effect. The 133 million Americans with preexisting conditions remain protected under the ACA. The 20 million Americans relying on the ACA for their health insurance also remain covered, at least for now.

As of 2019, Democrats control the U.S. House of Representatives. They may try to repair the many problems of the ACA, but can any such House bill ever pass the Senate, still controlled by Republicans, let alone ever be signed by the president? I'll just say to Republicans who shied away from supporting the popular ACA, be careful what you wish for; you just might "get it" in the 2020 election cycle.

Regulate Insurance and Drug Prices

Insurance and pharmaceutical price reform is a Sisyphean task. The healthcare industry, including the hospital conglomerates and physicians, resists changes. Money keeps things as they are.

Big Insurance, Big Pharma and Big Hospitals benefit from the system as it stands. I believe they are mostly concerned about how "the other" is charging too much, thereby making it harder for them to charge more for their own piece of the healthcare pie.

Robert Goff gave his views on hospitals and their profit system. Let me look at two other so-called "bad boys" in healthcare costs — insurance companies and pharmaceutical companies.

Health insurance company profits are booming. Bob Herman at Axios found the five largest U.S. insurance companies reported $4.5 billion in net earnings for the first quarter 2017. The insurers employ 2.5 million people. A robust industry with healthy margins.

In an NPR interview, Herman said that since Obamacare began, the cumulative salaries of insurance and pharma CEOs has tallied $9.8 billion. The top earner was John Martin, former CEO of Gilead Science, who took home in excess of $900 million.

You might think all of this quality brainpower would make great allies for reformers trying to bring about financial reforms to relieve the burdens carried by you and me. Not so. No motivation. Herman said executives are not paid to slow spending. Much of their pay is in stock or stock options. "Their incentive is to do whatever it takes to make that stock go up." Stock prices drives drug prices.

Raising prices to lift stock values is the opposite of what we need to heal our broken system. Why not try to lower prices, eliminate unnecessary care and drugs, and coordinate care better? In my view, none of the Republican and Democratic proposals really address the core causes of rising costs in our healthcare system.

An intriguing development is "health insurance on demand." Pioneering the concept, according to CNBC in 2018, is a startup in Minneapolis called Bind. Backed by UnitedHealthcare and partners, Bind uses data analytics to offer consumers "only the coverage they need, when they need it, without narrowing their network."

On-demand insurance is said to be more affordable. Without high deductibles, Bind covers preventive care, primary and specialty care, urgent or emergency care, hospital care, chronic care, and "pharmacy needs." Beyond its core, Bind offers coverage as needed, such as for pregnancy or cancer. Can on-demand insurance be a viable way to reduce medical debt?

This leads me to the drug industry. Among all the "out-of-control" health care sectors, the most widely attacked is the drug industry. Why the outrage?

Eric Reguly, European Bureau Chief for The Globe and Mail, wrote a scathing article, "Rx for Excess: The truth behind big pharma spending," He asked why prices of name-brand drugs keep soaring. His simple answer: "Because they can."

> 'Free market' economies shun limits on profits, so pricing regulations are unlikely.

Reguly alleges that both governments and consumers have been "brainwashed" into thinking all the double-digit price increases are necessary to fund world-class research and development programs, investing in inventing to make us healthier.

This rationale, apparently, allowed Gilead Sciences to charge $84,000 for a 12-week course of treatment (at about $1,000 a pill) for Sovaldi, their antiviral treatment for hepatitis C. Médecins Sans Frontières called the Gilead price "shocking," noting it would cost $227 billion to properly treat the 2.7 million Americans with hep C, "let alone the rest of the world."

Reguly labels the argument of "sumptuous prices for sumptuous R&D" a blatant fraud. What's really driving up drug prices are share buybacks and dividends, he said, naming Valeant Pharmaceuticals' CEO, Michael Pearson, who in 2018 saw the valuations of his stock holdings and options swell to almost $3 billion.

Can we reduce U.S. healthcare costs by regulating the profits of insurance and pharmaceutical companies? "Free market" economies shun limits on profits, so pricing regulations are unlikely.

Add Medicare Option to the ACA

People are making a strong argument for adding a "Medicare Option" to the ACA. This would offer a voluntary "opt-in" from age 50 (or 55) to 65, the age where Medicare starts today. Supplemental insurance would cover the 20 percent that Medicare does not cover (same as Medicare now). This would modestly expand Medicare.

The main Medicare Option bills now in congress are led by Sen. Debbie Stabenow (D-Mich.), who sees it starting at age 55, and Rep. Brian Higgins (D-NY), who wants it to start at age 50. The Stabenow and Higgins bills both rely on marketplace subsidies and employer participation. Both offer assurance that any Medicare buy-in would not compete with commercial marketplace plans.

No matter what form any Medicare Option takes, detractors will deride it as "creeping socialism." Never give a dog a bone, even with scant meat on it, and try to take it back. If Medicare and Social Security are socialist schemes to rot moral character and undermine personal responsibility? If so, which Americans would give it up?

Here's a point of reference. Imagine America 50 years ago when only 48 percent of all "senior citizens" had health insurance. About 35 percent of all seniors were living in poverty. The life expectancy for men was 66 years and 73 years for women. All that changed on July 30, 1965, with the passage of Medicare. Today, only two percent of us over age 65 lack healthcare coverage. Better yet, poverty among those of us age 65 and older has been reduced by two-thirds.

Now picture mature people from age 50 to 65 enjoying a similar improvement in their life and health. Is this politically viable? Picture a future United States of America in which everybody at age 50 enjoys all the benefits of Medicare, with little or no medical debt. I wonder, will the younger generations be a tad envious?

If you think it was painful trying to "repeal and (never) replace" Obamacare, imagine a "Medicare Option' bill inciting howls of protest from those younger and healthier taxpayers unwilling to pay for their ailing elders! Will they march on Washington, or will empathy reign?

A bipartisan Medicare Option could pass in the House, and it might pass in Senate if enough Republicans are willing. Is this the best solution for us? Do you prefer a more sweeping change?

> **Picture a future in which all people at age 50 enjoy the benefits of Medicare, with little or no medical debt.**

Medicare for All

A 2018 Reuters survey determined that 70 percent of Americans support "Medicare for All," the current popular title for single-payer healthcare. Reuters quoted Larry Levitt, senior vice president for health reform at the Kaiser Family Foundation, "The advantage of Medicare for All, which is much closer to how the rest of the world provides health care to their residents, is that you can achieve universal health care at a lower cost."

Joel Segal, co-author of the legislation, HR 676, "Expanded and Improved Medicare For All," lays out the three main advantages of such a proposed single payer solution:

- No out-of-pocket costs.
- No hospital or physician bills to pay.
- No more medical debt.

Patients, physicians and hospitals would make decisions based on the need to generate health, not the need of insurance companies and medical providers in business to generate profits.

Under HR 676, healthcare would be publicly financed, but privately operated, same as Medicare is now. Said Segal, "This is different from the 'socialized' national health system of medicine they have in England, or what we have here in America with the VA, where the government itself owns and operates the healthcare system."

Under HR 676, he added, as with Medicare now, "you would show your government card, receive care services and go home. As with Medicare now, you would not worry about bills to pay, or bill collectors if you can't pay."

> **Healthcare would be publicly financed, but privately operated, same as Medicare.**

Both of the proposed Medicare for All laws, one sponsored by Rep. Keith Ellison (D-MN), the other by Sen. Bernie Sanders (D-VT), would cut the current 12 percent rate of uninsured people to zero. Everyone would be enrolled into one plan without any deductibles or co-payments. No one could opt out.

People could still buy supplemental private health insurance, akin to the "Medigap" supplemental plans today. Unlike Medicare, there would be no age limits. All Americans would be fully covered from birth to grave. Apart from Medigap supplementals, all other form of private health coverage would vanish. Most of the existing public programs, including Medicare as it exists today, Medicaid, and CHIP, would be replaced. Healthcare financing would shift away from households and employers to the federal government.

Naturally, the proposal has enemies. Beyond the ideological or morality issues (in a number of quarters), critics raise the spectre of cost. The Mercatus Center in Virginia (Koch-funded) projected a $32.6 trillion increase in federal spending over ten years.

Sanders' answer: "If every major country on earth can guarantee health care to all and achieve better health outcomes while spending substantially less per capita than we do, it is absurd for anyone to suggest that the United States cannot do the same."

Universal Healthcare

Could universal health care for every person at any age cost less and save money? That depends on who you ask.

Physicians for a National Health Plan assert a national health insurance program would save at least $150 billion annually on just paperwork alone. Under private insurance today, they argue, more than 25 percent of every health care dollar earned by the insurance companies goes not for claims but for marketing, billing, utilization review, and duplication (what some call "waste").

The Peterson-Kaiser Health System Tracker reported that other wealthy countries, on average, spend half as much per person on healthcare as the USA. This means that $10,000 in care charges here are $5,000 "over there." Anybody with a capitalist bent ought to love a solution that costs less and saves money, but I guess that depends on the capitalist — and the circumstances.

Universal healthcare could offer a valuable social side-benefit: Equity in health care delivery. If universal healthcare or single-payer is constructed in such a fashion that my doctor is certifiably as good as your doctor, if our treatments are equal and my medicines are the same quality as yours, then we both have better health outcomes and a better quality of life ahead. We need not compete for our care. The healthcare system can focus on health not finance.

In Canada's single-payer system, said Newsweek, "Medicine is not a commodity to be sold to the highest bidder, but a right that must be distributed equitably to one and all, and (like the Canadian character) ferociously egalitarian, but thrifty at the same time."

Why do we Americans resist such a sensible, moral social value? Seems to me this is where Americans reveal a form of Stockholm Syndrome. As lifelong captives of "the system," we love our captors. We believe down is up.

To call single payer a moral issue, to say each citizen deserves equal access to quality healthcare, somehow turns advocates into something unamerican — socialists! Really? Forget the labels. What's right?

We Americans need to take a moral stand that health is a human right. I personally want our country to join the ranks of other enlightened nations.

> **Americans need to take a moral stand that health is a human right.**

The American Medical Debt Commission

I favor America no longer being a healthcare have-not nation. To get there, I'm learning to think outside my box thanks to Joel Segal, referred by a colleague in November 2018. In a long freeflow phone conversation, I learned he'd been senior legislative assistant to retired Rep. John Conyers, Chair of the Congressional Universal Health Care Task Force. Joel helped write the ACA. He shared with me his personal struggles with medical debt. As we explored our thoughts on healthcare in America, I had an "aha!" moment.

It's one thing to begin a charity that forgives medical debt, yet it's something else to grasp the tools for changing the law governing medical debt. Joel has been drafting laws for years. He has shaped public policy in practical ways that effect our daily lives. His efforts made me realize that RIP has been playing too small.

Showing what's possible, within days after we met, Joel drafted the "The American Medical Debt Commission Act of 2019."

Congress would establish an independent bipartisan "Medical Debt Commission that provides factual information on an annual basis to Congress and the general public on the medical debt crisis in America." A 25-member commission, chosen by the House Energy and Commerce Committee, would represent physicians, academics, hospital administrators, civil society organizations, local and state elected officials, foundations, think tanks, universities, medical debt experts, and patients impacted by medical debt.

The Commission would convene four times a year. Their tasks would include publishing an annual report about America's medical debt crisis, available for download at the website of the Centers for Medicare & Medicaid Services. The report would offer Commission recommendations on how to address the medical debt crisis with the broadest possible spectrum of solutions, based on best practices, to end the medical debt crisis.

At least once a year, Commission members would appear before the House committee to testify about the status of the U.S. medical debt crisis, reporting facts and results from the various attempted solutions addressing U.S. medical debt.

Joel could rapidly draft such a bill because he knows how to do it. He has an enviable record of crafting bills that actually get passed. Joel's mastery of the legislative process sparked in me a vision of the bold and audacious world in which I want to live — where we go beyond complaining about problems to actually solving them.

Not in Conclusion, in Anticipation

By the time this book was published in December 2018, RIP had forgiven almost $500 million in medical debt for about 250,000 individuals and families. Double that amount is now in our pipeline. Laudable, but we do not delude ourselves. We are only "sweeping up after the parade." I am increasingly convinced our deeper purpose is awakening America to the problem of medical debt and galvanizing us into action. I hope this book adds to the public awakening.

Most Americans already know our current healthcare system is broken. Despite the bash-label of "socialism" and the tired bleat of "we can't afford it," we Americans want full healthcare coverage for ourselves and our families with no more medical debt.

We Americans somehow cough up enough in taxes now to support the protections provided by our military, our police and our fire departments.

> **Americans want full healthcare coverage for ourselves and our families with no more medical debt.**

The same willingness to be taxed needs to happen for the protection of our health, which for me means universal healthcare. We accept the tax burden for Medicare and Social Security, even if we grumble about it. When we get older and we depend on Medicare and Social Security, we fee grateful that we and others paid our taxes.

Can enough of us educate ourselves out of fearful hopelessness, investigate our healthcare alternatives and choose new solutions?

Hippocrates wrote, "Before you heal someone, ask him [her] if he's willing to give up the things that made him sick." Medical debt is making Americans sick and poor. Are we willing to give it up?

To realize America's founding promise of "Life, liberty, and the pursuit of happiness," let's notice the order these words appear. Life, which depends on health, comes first. Without health, liberty has little value, and the pursuit of happiness is meaningless. Whenever our vote is cast, America's health needs to come first.

"If you have your health, you have everything," goes the saying. Let's stop depriving ourselves of that everything.

End medical debt.

*Hope lies in dreams, in imagination,
and in the courage of those who dare
to make dreams into reality.*

— JONAS SALK, M.D

About the Authors

Jerry Ashton — Jerry has more than 40 years of experience in the credit and collections industry. In 1995, to uplift the way debtors are treated, he formed CFO Advisors in New York. His teams serviced a half billion in receivables for Fortune 500 companies. Inspired by Occupy Wall Street's "Rolling Jubilee" debt forgiveness campaign, he joined with Craig Antico, his CFO partner, to found RIP Medical Debt. Jerry serves as RIP's Education and Outreach Director.

Robert Goff — Retired from 40 years in the healthcare industry, Robert E. Goff is a respected consultant in care delivery, organization and financing. His senior leadership roles include hospital administrator, regulator, managed care executive, association executive, educator, and entrepreneur. He developed one of the first for-profit HMOs in New York State. He was the head of the University Physicians Network. Robert is RIP's founding board member.

Craig Antico — A financial industry leader in collections, debt buying, outsourcing, and consulting, Craig's 30-year career features work with IBM, Johnson & Johnson, collection agencies, and medical distributors. An expert in data analytics, he early joined the distressed debt exchange, eDebt. He joined Jerry at CFO Advisors and as a founder of RIP Medical Debt. Craig serves as RIP's Operations Director.

"Do not accustom yourself to consider debt only as an inconvenience; you will find it a calamity.

— Samuel Johnson

About RIP Medical Debt

RIP Medical Debt is a 501(c)(3) not-for-profit national charity based in New York, incorporated in 2014, which locates, buys and forgives unpayable medical debt for those burdened by financial hardship.

RIP to date has abolished $500 million in medical debt for about 250,000 Americans. They support communities across the country in conducting local medical debt forgiveness campaigns. They have a special interest in forgiving the medical debt of veterans.

RIP buys large batches of medical billing accounts in "portfolios" for about a penny on the dollar, so donations to RIP deliver "a lot of bang for the buck." A $100 donation can forgive $10,000 in debt.

RIP cannot yet forgive medical debt for individuals on request, but people in need can apply for future debt relief at the RIP website by joining the Debt Forgiveness Registry.

Surprised people who receive in the mail a yellow RIP envelope enjoy no tax consequences from the charitable gift. Debt forgiveness from RIP is a freely given "random act of kindness."

For more information, visit RIPmedicaldebt.org

Medical debts are the number-one cause of bankruptcy in America.

— BARBARA EHRENREICH

CPSIA information can be obtained
at www.ICGtesting.com
Printed in the USA
BVHW031647140419
545389BV00001B/1/P